D0943554

Stuart Yarnold

Windows 7
Tips & Techniques

In easy steps is an imprint of In Easy Steps Limited
Southfield Road · Southam
Warwickshire CV47 0FB · United Kingdom
www.ineasysteps.com

Copyright © 2010 by In Easy Steps Limited. All rights reserved. No part of this book may be reproduced or transmitted in any form or by any means, electronic or mechanical, including photocopying, recording, or by any information storage or retrieval system, without prior written permission from the publisher.

Notice of Liability
Every effort has been made to ensure that this book contains accurate and current information. However, In Easy Steps Limited and the author shall not be liable for any loss or damage suffered by readers as a result of any information contained herein.

Trademarks
Microsoft® and Windows® are registered trademarks of Microsoft Corporation. All other trademarks are acknowledged as belonging to their respective companies.

In Easy Steps Limited supports The Forest Stewardship Council (FSC), the leading international forest certification organisation. All our titles that are printed on Greenpeace approved FSC certified paper carry the FSC logo.

Mixed Sources
Product group from well-managed forests and other controlled sources
www.fsc.org Cert no. SGS-COC-005998
© 1996 Forest Stewardship Council

FSC

Printed and bound in the United Kingdom

ISBN 978-1-84078-388-9

Contents

31143009828881
005.446 Yarnold, S
Yarnold, Stuart.
Windows 7 tips & techniques /

Main

8   Installation/Setting Up   113

9   Shortcuts   125

10   Facts and Figures   135

11   The Internet   149

1 Performance

Windows 7, as new users will soon discover, takes a heavy toll on a PC's resources. Those of you whose systems are struggling to run this new operating system will be able to achieve a much higher level of performance by implementing the measures described in this chapter. We also explain some more general performance-boosting steps.

Introduction

Early versions of Windows – 95, 98, and to a lesser degree, Me – were relatively simple operating systems that would run fine on virtually all PCs. They didn't require anything out of the ordinary with regard to hardware.

The introduction of Windows XP changed that, and for the first time many users were faced with the prospect of upgrading their PC's hardware in order to get the operating system to run properly. Even so, in the main, this involved no more than increasing the amount of memory in the system – a relatively simple procedure.

Windows Vista, and now Windows 7, have taken the issue of hardware requirements to a different level. This is the first thing that users new to Windows 7 have to consider. To achieve a performance level that is satisfactory for typical PC uses, many more people than was the case with XP will have to upgrade their system's hardware. In order to get the maximum performance from Windows 7, the majority of current XP users will need to upgrade to some degree. However, users upgrading from Vista will not need to do so as hardware requirements for Windows 7 are similar to Vista.

Unfortunately, the upgrades most likely to be needed – memory and video – involve opening up the system case; something the typical user may balk at, not to mention the cost involved.

However, out-of-the-box, Windows 7 is configured for optimal appearance rather than performance. This means that there are quite a few adjustments that can be made to the default settings, which will make it run considerably faster. For the many users whose hardware provides a performance level that is on the borderline between poor and acceptable, these can negate the need for a hardware upgrade.

There are also some more general steps that users can take in order to keep their system running, not just at peak performance but also reliably. These are not specific to Windows 7; they apply to any operating system.

This chapter shows you the tweaks that can be made to Windows 7's default settings to improve its performance, and also shows, generally, how to keep your PC running smoothly and reliably.

Hot tip

To get the best out of Windows 7, you will need a powerful system. While it will run on medium-specification PCs, its full capabilities won't be seen.

Don't forget

If your system is struggling with Windows 7, there are some steps you can take to reduce the demands made by it.

Add More Memory

Without any doubt, the quickest and most effective method of improving the overall performance of a computer is to simply increase the amount of memory it has.

Windows 7 will not function well with any less than 1 GB of memory. Optimum performance will require 2 GB.

So how do you go about doing this? It is in fact, a very simple procedure that takes no more than a few minutes but does require the system case to be opened. Once this has been done, you will see a large circuit board facing you at the right-hand side of the case. This is the motherboard and at the top-right, you will see the memory sockets containing the memory modules as shown below:

Open the retaining clips and insert the new module by pressing down on the top edge until the retaining clips close automatically

If one or more of the sockets are empty all you have to do is fit extra modules to complement the existing ones. If the sockets are all in use, you will have to remove some, or all, of the modules and replace them with modules of a larger capacity.

However, if the prospect of meddling inside the case doesn't appeal to you there is an easier, although less effective, option available. This is called ReadyBoost and is explained on page 10.

This is called ReadyBoost and is explained on page 10.

Hot tip

To find out how much memory your PC has, right-click the My Computer icon on the Start menu and then click Properties. Memory capacity will be detailed in the System section.

Don't forget

You cannot install just any memory - it has to be compatible. Consult your PC's manual to see which type you need.

Hot tip

Memory modules must be handled very carefully. Before touching one, ground yourself by touching the metal case chassis. If you don't, the electrostatic electricity in your body could well damage it.

Quick Speed Boost

Beware

ReadyBoost will not work with just any flash drive – it must be a good quality USB 2 model.

If Windows were to run out of memory, the PC would literally grind to a halt. To prevent this, it uses a Paging file on the hard drive as a memory substitute. The problem with this is that hard drives are much slower than memory, so performance is reduced when the Paging file is being used.

The solution is to prevent Windows having to use the Paging file, and the way to do this is to install more memory. However, many users don't know how to install memory; plus, it is expensive.

ReadyBoost provides a simple and cheap alternative. All you need is a USB 2 flash drive with a capacity of between 256 MB and 4 GB. Plug the drive into a USB port and Windows will automatically install it. Then the following window will pop up:

Don't forget

ReadyBoost enables you to increase your system's performance without having to buy and install more memory. It is also a much cheaper option as flash drives are half the price of memory of equivalent capacity.

1 Click "Speed up my system"

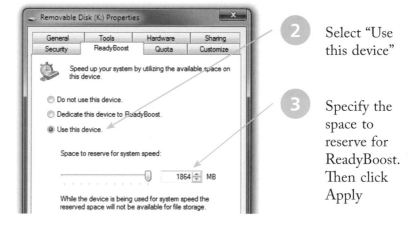

2 Select "Use this device"

3 Specify the space to reserve for ReadyBoost. Then click Apply

Hot tip

The minimum amount of flash memory you can use for ReadyBoost is 256 MB. The maximum amount is 4 GB. We suggest at least 1GB.

Windows will now use the USB drive as a cache for the most commonly paged data. The Paging file will still be on the hard drive but will be used much less.

Users with less than 1 GB of physical memory will benefit considerably by using ReadyBoost.

Aero is Cool but ...

While the Aero interface with its translucent window frames is undoubtedly attractive, it does place a considerable load on a PC's video system. Therefore, disabling Aero is one of the first things users, whose systems are struggling with Windows 7, should try.

Do it as follows:

1 Right-click the Desktop and click Personalize

2 The "Personalization" dialog box will open

3 Scroll down to "Basic and High Contrast Themes"

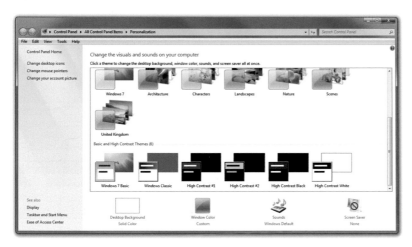

Hot tip

Don't forget about the old Windows Classic interface. This is still available in Windows 7 and while visually it is outdated, it is just as efficient.

Many users who use their PCs purely for work still prefer it.

4 Deselect Aero by selecting a different option, such as "Windows 7 Basic"

Your computer won't look nearly as flashy as before but it should be considerably more responsive. Also, as it is so easy to enable/disable Aero, it is quite practical to disable it only when you are running a resource-intensive application (a PC game, for example) that the system is struggling to cope with. When back to run-of-the-mill applications, you can enable it again.

Less is Sometimes Better

Windows 7 comes with a number of visual effects, e.g. fading or sliding menus, drop shadows, pointer shadows, etc. These are all designed to improve the look and feel of the Windows interface.

They do, however, add nothing to its functionality. In fact, they can, and do, have a negative impact on the system. Remember: each of these effects consumes system resources.

Users interested in performance rather than appearance will benefit from disabling some, or even all, of these essentially unnecessary graphic enhancements.

Hot tip

Windows 7's visual effects are purely cosmetic and serve no practical purpose. Disabling them will have no effect on the PC's functionality.

1 Go to Start, Control Panel, System, Advanced system settings

2 Click the Settings button under Performance

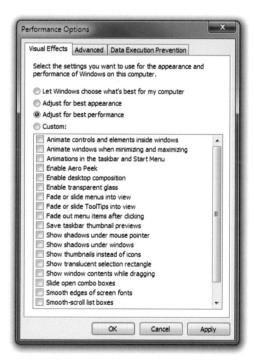

Beware

Disabling all of the effects will have a significant impact on the appearance of the Windows interface.

On the Visual Effects tab you will see a list of all Windows visual effects, plus several user options. By default, Windows chooses the second option "Adjust for best appearance", which enables all the effects. To disable them all, select "Adjust for best performance" as shown above. Alternatively, you can disable them individually.

Icon Thumbnails

By default, Windows 7 displays all file icons as thumbnails (mini graphical representations). This is particularly useful when viewing image files, as it enables you to see the image without having to first open it in an imaging program as shown below:

Don't forget

Graphic files are the slowest type of file to load. While icon thumbnails may be very small, because there are so many of them, they have a cumulative effect.

However, there is a downside. Because graphic files take longer to open than any other type of file, having this feature enabled does adversely affect system performance. Users who want their system to run as fast as possible, and those whose systems are struggling with Windows 7, will gain a boost in speed by disabling this feature. Do it as described below:

1 Go to Start, Control Panel, Folder Options. Then click the View tab

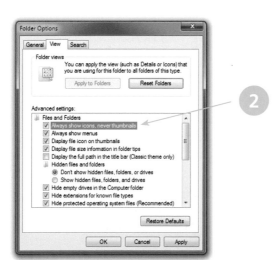

2 Check the "Always show icons, never thumbnails" check box

Hot tip

Another effect of disabling icon thumbnails is that folder icons will load more quickly.

13

Faster Paging

When Windows runs out of physical memory, it uses a special file on the hard drive as a substitute, known as the Paging file. Moving it to a different drive speeds up the paging operation, and thus system performance (see top margin note). To carry out this procedure you will, of course, need two hard drives.

Hot tip

A separate drive that doesn't have Windows and other applications installed on it, will be more responsive as it is used much less than the main drive. So placing the Paging file on it will improve the speed of the paging operation.

Hot tip

Creating a dedicated partition (see pages 117-118) of about 2 GB, specifically for the Paging file, will prevent it from becoming fragmented. This increases its performance further.

Hot tip

There is no benefit to be gained by moving the Paging file to a different partition on the main drive. It must be moved to a separate drive.

14

1. Go to Start, Control Panel, System. Click System Protection and then the Advanced tab

2. Click Settings (under Performance) and then the Advanced tab. Under Virtual Memory, click Change

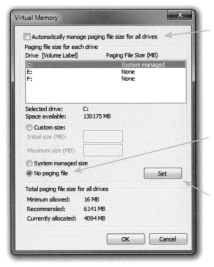

3. Uncheck "Automatically manage paging file size for all drives"

4. Select "No paging file"

5. Click Set. Ignore the warning message and click Yes

6. Select a different drive

7. Select "System managed size"

8. Click Set and then OK. Reboot for the change to take effect

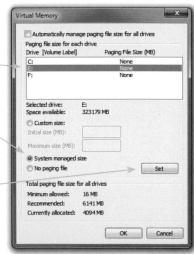

SuperFetch

The SuperFetch feature in Windows 7 helps to keep the computer consistently responsive to your programs by making better use of the computer's memory.

Windows SuperFetch prioritizes the programs you're currently using over background tasks, and also adapts to the way you work by tracking the programs you use most often and preloading these into memory. As a result, they open much more quickly when accessed.

On PCs that have 2 GB or more of memory, SuperFetch works very well. However, if your PC has less than 2 GB it can lead to excessive disk thrashing (see margin note) and sluggish system performance. The less memory you have, the worse the effect.

If you find yourself in this position, you have three options:

1) Upgrade your memory so you have at least 2 GB
2) Enable ReadyBoost
3) Disable the SuperFetch feature

The latter is done as follows:

Go to Start, Control Panel, Administrative Tools. Click Services and scroll down to the SuperFetch service.

Disk thrashing occurs on PCs that are low on memory. As a result, the operating system has to utilize the hard drive as a memory substitute. This leads to data being constantly transferred between the hard drive and the physical memory.

When this happens, the drive's indicator light will blink on and off continuously.

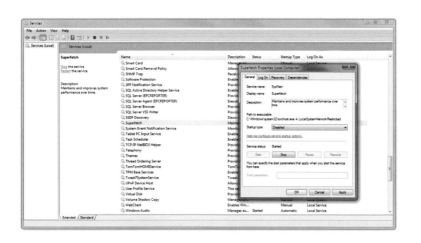

Double-click SuperFetch and in the Startup type drop-down box, select Disabled

Beware

Disk thrashing can damage or cause premature failure of the hard drive due to excessive wear and tear on the read/write heads.

Cancel Unneeded Services

Hot tip

Services that can be disabled are:

- IKE and AuthIP IPsec Keying Modules
- Remote Registry
- UPnP Device Host
- WebClient
- Windows Error Reporting Service
- Windows Image Acquisition (WIA)

If you don't use your PC for networking, the following can also be disabled:

- Computer Browser
- Distributed Link Tracking Client
- Net Logon
- Network Access Protection Agent
- Peer Name Resolution Protocol
- Peer Networking Identity Manager
- PnP-X IP Bus Enumerator
- SSDP Discovery
- Server
- TCP/IP NetBIOS Helper
- Workstation

When a Windows 7 PC is being used, in the background and unseen by the user, a number of applications known as Services will be running. While many of them are essential for certain functions of the operating system, there are some that are not.

As every running application makes a hit on system performance, this is something you do not want to be happening. Fortunately, you can override Windows and make the decision yourself as to which services should be running. As a guide, the services specified in the list on the left can be disabled safely. Do this as follows:

1 Go to Start, Control Panel, Administrative Tools. Click Services

2 Double-click the service to be disabled

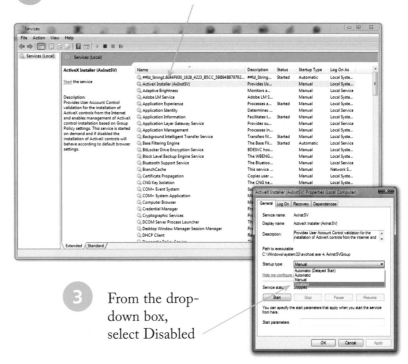

3 From the drop-down box, select Disabled

Should you consider disabling any services that are not listed on this page, we suggest that you first take a look at what the service does and also what other applications may be depending on it. This is explained on the next page.

1 Open the service's Properties dialog box. A description of the service's function is displayed here

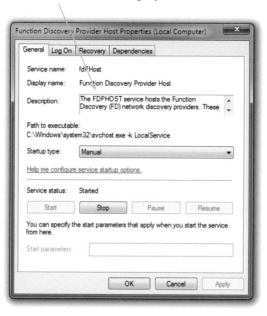

Hot tip

Be aware that some third-party applications add their own services. These can be disabled as well.

2 Click the Dependencies tab to see what other applications depend on the service

Don't forget

The Dependencies tab gives you forewarning of what will happen if you stop a particular service. For this reason, it is important to take a look here prior to making any changes.

Streamline the Registry

The registry is a central hierarchical database that holds all the important Windows settings regarding software, hardware and system configuration. It also provides a common location for all applications to save their launching parameters and data.

Over time, as the user installs and deletes programs, creates shortcuts and changes system settings, etc., obsolete and invalid key information builds up in the registry. While this does not have a major impact on a PC's performance, it can be the cause of system and program errors that can lead to instability issues.

The solution is to scan the registry periodically with a suitable application that will locate all the invalid entries and delete them.

While Windows Registry Editor is adequate for editing purposes, it does not provide a cleaning option. However, there are many of these applications available for download from the Internet. A typical example is Registry Mechanic (shown below). These programs provide various options, such as full or selective scans, backups, the creation of System Restore points, etc.

Beware

Changes to the registry can be dangerous. So create a system restore point using System Restore first. If you have any problems as a result of the change, you will be able to undo it by restoring the system.

Hot tip

We recommend you clean the registry about once a month. However, if you frequently install and uninstall software, change system settings, etc., it will be worth doing it more often.

Despite the operating system having been installed for just two weeks on this PC, Registry Mechanic found 179 problems (minor ones, admittedly)

Occasional use of a registry cleaner will help to keep your system stable and thus, more reliable.

Optimize the Hard Drive

There are several measures that can be taken to get the best out of this device and thus improve system performance.

Defragment the Hard Drive

Fragmentation is a term used to describe the process where files saved to a magnetic disk drive have their data split up on different parts of the disk, or disks, instead of being stored contiguously. When a fragmented file is accessed, the drive's read/write heads have to hunt about to locate all of the different parts of the file before they can be reassembled in the original form. The result is that the file will take much longer to open than it should do, and the system will be sluggish.

To address this issue, Windows provides a tool called Disk Defragmenter. This application "undoes" the fragmentation by rearranging the data on the disk so that each file is stored as a complete unit. You can access Windows Disk Defragmenter by going to Start, All Programs, Accessories, System Tools.

Beware

A badly fragmented drive will have a major impact on your system's performance. For this reason, never disable the defragmenting utility.

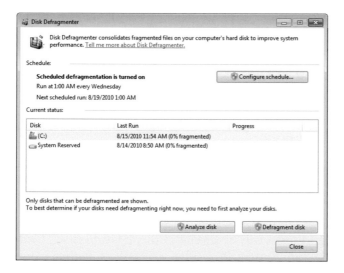

Beware

When you run Disk Defragmenter, make sure that no other applications are open, as they may interfere with the defragmention procedure.

By default, it is set to run once a week, which for normal usage is quite adequate. However, if you use the PC on a daily basis, or are constantly creating, deleting, modifying or moving files, we suggest you change the default setting to Daily.

To do this, click the Configure Schedule button and from the drop-down list, select Daily. From here, you can also set the time of the scheduled defragment.

...cont'd

Keep it Lean and Mean

When approximately 70 per cent of a hard drive's storage capacity has been used, its performance level will start to decrease. It will also be more likely to be affected by the issue of fragmentation.

So when it begins to approach this mark, you should start thinking about freeing up some space. As it's a sure fact that many of the files on your drive will be redundant, you can usually do this without losing anything important.

1 Go to Start, All Programs, Accessories, System Tools and click Disk Cleanup

Beware

The more data you have on your drive, the worse the effects of fragmentation.

2 Under Files to delete, you will see a list of all the files that can be safely deleted. Check all the boxes and then click OK to delete them

The next thing to delete is System Restore points. As these are actually system backups, they are very large files, often several GBs in size, and there will be several of them. Go to Start, Control Panel, System, System Protection. Click the Configure Button and then click the "Delete all restore points ..." button. Click OK and then back in the System Protection dialog box, create a new (single) restore point by clicking the Create button.

Don't forget

System Restore points are created whenever major changes are made to the system. These points can occupy a tremendous amount of disk space, so deleting them is worth doing.

Finally, open the Programs and Features utility in the Control Panel. Here, you'll see a list of all the programs installed on the PC. Go through it and uninstall any that you don't use.

You'll now have a more responsive drive, plus more disk space.

Keep the File System Healthy

Over time, especially if the PC is well-used, file system and data faults can build up on the hard drive. Not only can these have an adverse effect on the PC's performance, they can also be the cause of general system instability, and thus potential loss of data.

To correct these types of faults, Windows provides a disk maintenance utility called Chkdsk. Access it as follows:

1 Open My Computer and right-click the hard drive. Click Properties and then the Tools tab

 Hot tip

Make a point of running Chkdsk on a regular basis. In particular, be sure to run it after every incorrect shutdown or system crash. These are the actions that will introduce file system errors to the hard drive.

If you don't do this, one of these days your system will simply refuse to boot up.

2 Under Error-checking, click the Check Now button

3 Check "Automatically fix file system errors." Then click Start

Note that running Chkdsk on the drive on which Windows is installed will require a system reboot. With all other drives, the procedure is usually done within the Windows interface.

22

Hot tip

A RAID 0 configuration splits the data across the drives. As each drive handles half the workload, data transfer rates are improved considerably. The downside is that if either of the drives fail, all the PC's data will be lost.

Hot tip

A RAID 1 configuration copies data to each drive. The advantage here is security – if one drive fails, the data is recoverable from the other one. The drawback is that the capacity of one of the drives is lost.

Hot tip

A RAID 0/1 configuration is basically a combination of RAID 0 and RAID 1. It offers the benefits of both but requires at least four hard drives.

RAID Span is merely a way of combining two drives into one – there's no real benefit from it.

Hard Drive Speed Boost

This tip shows how to boost hard drive speed, and thus system performance, by implementing a hard drive configuration technology known as RAID (Redundant Array of Independent Disks). This is a way of configuring a combination of hard drives to gain specific benefits; in this case, an increase in drive speed.

To set up a RAID configuration, you will need two hard drives and a RAID controller. With regard to the latter, most modern motherboards provide one; check your motherboard documentation to see if yours does – if so, you're all set. If it doesn't, you'll need to buy a RAID controller PCI card, which you install in a PCI slot on the motherboard.

When you have installed the second hard drive, boot the PC and then press the key specified in the motherboard documentation to open the RAID setup utility.

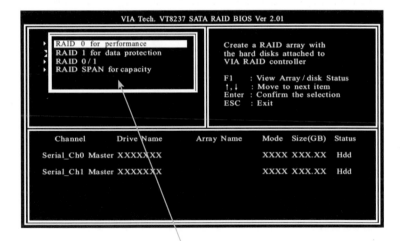

Typically, you will be given four options: RAID 0, RAID 1, RAID 0/1 and RAID Span – see margin notes.

To make the task easier, most RAID setup utilities offer an Auto-setup option. All you have to do is specify the configuration required, which in this case is RAID 0. The utility will then set up the configuration automatically; the process taking only a few seconds. Reboot and you're done.

Go to My Computer and you will see just one drive. Its capacity however, will be the combined capacities of the two drives.

Update Device Drivers

First, what exactly is a driver? Well, let's assume that you are about to print a document and have opened your printer software to change a few settings. What you are looking at is actually a driver, in this case your printer's driver.

A driver has three purposes. Some, like the printer driver mentioned above, act as an interface between the device and the user, allowing changes to be made to the way the device operates.

Second, all drivers act as an interface between their device and the operating system. They tell the operating system what the device needs in terms of system resources for correct operation.

Third, drivers provide a way for hardware manufacturers to update their devices to take account of advances in technology, both hardware and software.

Unfortunately, drivers can cause problems, particularly when they are used with a new operating system (this invariably introduces technologies that the drivers' devices were not designed for). In most cases they will install without problems and the devices will appear to be functioning. However, behind the scenes they may well be the cause of incompatibility issues that can lead to both instability and loss of system performance.

In an effort to prevent this, Windows displays a warning message when it detects that a potentially problematic driver is being installed, as shown below. However, it is a fact that most users ignore these messages and install the driver regardless.

If you've done this yourself, you should be aware that you may well have compromised your system.

So to be quite sure that the PC is running at its best, you must uninstall all non-certified Windows drivers (see margin note) and replace them with ones that are. Do this as described on the next page.

Hot tip

Upgrading your device drivers is not just important with regard to the operating system. In most cases, the devices themselves will perform better as a result.

Hot tip

Drivers that are certified for use with Windows have been tested by Windows Hardware Quality Labs (WHQL). They are commonly referred to as "signed drivers" as they have been digitally tagged as such.

...cont'd

1 Click Start and then in the search box type "verifier". Press Enter to open the Driver Verifier Manager

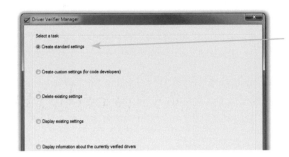

2 Select "Create Standard Settings" and click Next

Hot tip

Many users assume that system crashes and lockups are due to faults in the operating system. The reality is that the majority of them are caused by either uncertified hardware drivers or by low quality memory.

3 In the next dialog box, select "Automatically select unsigned drivers" and click Next

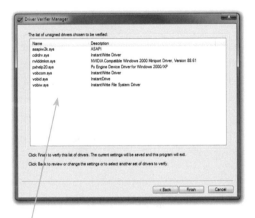

4 In the final dialog box, you will see a list of all the unsigned drivers on the PC

While they are probably OK, these drivers are all potential causes of system problems. Therefore, if you want to be absolutely certain that your computer is stable, and performing as well as possible, you will have to either replace them all with Windows certified (signed) versions, or uninstall them.

To this end, visit the websites of the manufacturers of the devices and look for updated drivers certified for use with Windows 7. Download and install them. If a manufacturer doesn't provide a Windows 7 driver, ideally you should replace the device with one from a manufacturer that does.

Prioritize CPU Resources

"Priority" is the measure that Windows uses to determine the amount of CPU time that each application receives. By default, most applications are set to the Normal priority level, so by changing a specific program to a higher level you can effectively boost its performance. This is useful when you are using several applications simultaneously (multi-tasking).

Do the following:

1. Run the program to be prioritized

2. Open the Task Manager (Ctrl+Shift+Esc)

3. Click the Processes tab and locate your application. Right-click it and select the desired Priority setting

Note that changes to priority level are not permanent; they are effective only while the program is running. If you close it and then open it again, it will have reverted to the default setting.

Beware

The highest priority setting is Realtime. This will give an application the same priority as critical system services.

We recommended that you do not use this, as doing so can render your system unstable.

Hot tip

You can also set lower priority levels for your applications. For example, if you have an open program that is accessed infrequently, giving it a lower priority will increase the CPU resources available for more frequently used applications.

Third-Party Software

Having tweaked Windows to give maximum performance, you should now look at your PC's applications. These can also be the cause of performance issues.

Program Overload

The first thing to examine is the amount of programs you have installed. The more there are the slower your PC is going to be, even if they are not being used. If this puzzles you, be aware that many applications (or parts of) run unseen in the background.

A typical example is CD/DVD authoring programs: these usually install a virtual CD driver that runs even when the program is closed. Many other programs do the same sort of thing. So the more software you install, inevitably the more of these background applications there will be. Not only do they slow system performance, they also affect shut down and startup speeds. So open the Programs and Features utility in the Control Panel and uninstall all the programs you can live without. Your system will be more responsive afterwards.

Resource Hogs

Certain types of application are well known for having a major impact on a PC's performance. Antivirus and system utility programs are two of the worst offenders.

To be effective, the former must monitor much of what's going on in the PC and so, inevitably, they slow the system down by a considerable degree. Probably most users consider this to be a price worth paying in order to keep their system clean.

However, it is a fact that you only need to have an antivirus program running for the following activities:

- When you are connected to the Internet
- When you are opening an email (online or offline)
- When a removable disk (floppy, CD/DVD) is run
- When a drive is added to the system

These are the ways that viruses get on to a user's PC. If you are connected to the Internet, even if you aren't using it, you must have an antivirus program running. The same applies when opening emails. However, if you aren't doing any of the above, you can safely close your antivirus program. Doing so will give your system a noticeable boost in speed.

Hot tip

It must be mentioned here that many antivirus programs released in the last year or so have considerably less impact on system performance than previous versions did. However, if yours is older than this, the comments on this page apply.

With regard to system utilities (an example being Norton Utilities), many people use these to maintain their system. They offer various functions to the user – diagnostics, repair, system tuning, maintenance, etc. Many of these tools can be run as needed and then turned off when finished with, which is fine. Others however, such as disk monitoring tools that run permanently in the background, can be a real drain on resources and will make a serious impact on the PC's performance.

Our advice is to not use this type of program at all, as Windows 7 provides you with all the tools you need to keep your system in good shape. If you must use them, at least avoid the monitoring applications and instead, just use those that can be run when needed and then turned off.

Malware

Malware is a term that encompasses invasive software, such as adware, spyware and browser hijackers. Quite apart from compromising your PC's security and intruding on your privacy, they can also slow your Internet activities considerably and, in the case of hijackers, can have a real impact on the PC's performance.

Windows 7's answer to this problem is the Windows Defender utility, which is enabled by default. In theory, this application should keep your system clean of all malware. In practice, however, it is unlikely to do so. Just as email spammers are constantly devising new ways to circumvent spam filters and other safeguards, the authors of malware software are doing the same with anti-malware programs.

You have two ways to approach this problem: prevention or cure. To prevent malware getting on to your PC, never do any of the following:

- Download anything from the Internet unless you are quite sure about the source
- Browse the Internet with any of Internet Explorer's security features turned off
- Install software from unverifiable sources

If you must do any of the above, or already have, scan your system not just with Windows Defender, but also with Ad-Aware and Spybot Search & Destroy (see margin note).

Don't forget

Many of the tools provided by utility programs are superior to the tools bundled with Windows. Use these by all means; just avoid the system and hard drive monitoring tools that run permanently in the background.

Hot tip

No anti-malware program is perfect, so to ensure your system is as clean as possible, we suggest you also use Ad-Aware (available from www.lavasoftusa. com) and Spybot Search & Destroy (available from www.safer-networking. org). These are two of the best anti-malware applications and free versions of both can be downloaded.

Spring-Clean the PC

There comes a time in the life of any well-used computer when it will benefit hugely from a good clear out. Over time, as files are created and deleted, programs are installed and uninstalled, the inevitable crashes occur, and users do things they shouldn't. A PC can become literally clogged up with redundant and useless data, long-forgotten files, programs, and broken shortcuts. Also, essential system or program files may have gone missing or been corrupted, leading to all manner of niggling little faults and problems. The result is a marked decrease in system performance.

There is absolutely nothing that can be done about this, no matter how carefully you maintain the PC; it is as inevitable as night following day.

So what's the answer? In short, scrap the lot and start again from scratch. This doesn't mean throwing away the computer and buying a new one, but rather junking all the data that's inside it.

The method of doing this is known as formatting and this procedure will purge the hard drive of all its data. Then you install a new copy of the operating system, reinstall your devices and then all your programs. The result will be a PC that is, to all intents and purposes, brand-new. Instead of chugging and spluttering along, it will now roar, much as an old car will if fitted with a new engine.

Beware

Installing a new copy of Windows over the old one is not as effective as a clean installation.
   While it will repair many faults in Windows itself, it may not repair them all, nor will it repair corrupted third-party software or get rid of malware. Many problems will remain.

Hot tip

Having restored your PC to an "as new" condition, we suggest you use Windows 7's Backup utility to create a mirror image of the system on a separate partition or hard drive. In future, you will be able to fully restore your PC in about ten minutes as opposed to the several hours it would take otherwise.

1 Make a backup of any data you wish to keep. Things to include are: email messages, email contacts, Internet Favorites, passwords, and your documents and graphics. To assist in making your backup, Windows 7 provides you with a Backup utility (see page 104). Then make a backup of your system's settings with Windows 7's Windows Easy Transfer utility (see page 120)

2 Do a clean installation of Windows as described on pages 115-116

3 Reinstall your hardware devices, system settings, applications, and finally your data

Your PC will now be like a brand-new machine.

2 Startup and Shutdown

Don't you just hate it when your PC insists on taking its own sweet time to start up and shut down. The procedures described in this chapter will teach it some manners and ensure that its laggardly ways are a thing of the past.

Quick Boot

When a computer is booted, the BIOS checks and initializes the system's hardware. Having done this, it then searches all the drives for the operating system. By default, it will look in the floppy drive first, then the hard drive and finally the CD/DVD drive.

This tip ensures that it goes immediately to the right drive, i.e. the hard drive, thus saving time.

1 Start the PC and when you see text on the screen, press the key needed to enter the BIOS setup program (see bottom margin note)

2 Using the arrow keys, open the Advanced BIOS Features page and press Enter

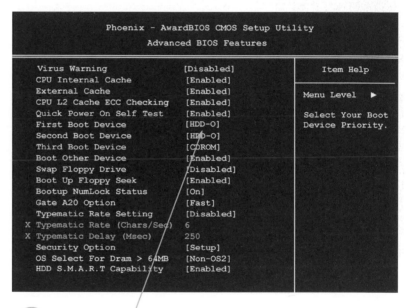

3 Scroll to First Boot Device and using the Page Up/Page Down keys, cycle through the options and select HDD-0

Note that the description above (and on page 33) relates to an AWARD BIOS. Users with BIOSs from other manufacturers will find that the terminology used, and page layouts, differ slightly.

Hot tip

The BIOS is a chip on the motherboard that contains a software program. This handles the routines necessary to boot the PC.

Don't forget

The key needed to enter the BIOS setup program will be specified at the bottom of the first boot screen. With AWARD BIOSs, it is usually Delete, and with AMI BIOSs, F2. It will also be specified in the PC's manual.

BIOS Speed Boost

Every BIOS has a diagnostic utility called the Power On Self Test (POST), which checks that vital parts of the system, such as the video and memory, are functioning correctly. If there is a problem, it will warn the user accordingly in the form of a series of coded beeps or an error message.

However, the BIOS can be configured to skip through certain non-essential parts of the POST, thus speeding up boot time considerably.

1. In the BIOS setup program, open the Advanced BIOS Features page

31

Hot tip

This setting has various names depending on the BIOS manufacturer. Examples are: "perform quick memory test," "quick boot," "quick power on self test," etc.

```
             Phoenix - AwardBIOS CMOS Setup Utility
                    Advanced BIOS Features

    Virus Warning              [Disabled]         Item Help
    CPU Internal Cache         [Enabled]
    External Cache             [Enabled]      Menu Level   ▶
    CPU L2 Cache ECC Checking  [Enabled]
    Quick Power On Self Test   [Enabled]      Select Your Boot
    First Boot Device          [HDD-0]        Device Priority.
    Second Boot Device         [HDD-0]
    Third Boot Device          [CDROM]
    Boot Other Device          [Enabled]
    Swap Floppy Drive          [Disabled]
    Boot Up Floppy Seek        [Enabled]
    Bootup NumLock Status      [On]
    Gate A20 Option            [Fast]
    Typematic Rate Setting     [Disabled]
  X Typematic Rate (Chars/Sec) 6
  X Typematic Delay (Msec)     250
    Security Option            [Setup]
    OS Select For Dram > 64MB  [Non-OS2]
    HDD S.M.A.R.T Capability   [Enabled]
```

2. Scroll to Quick Power On Self Test and select Enabled

Amongst other things, this will make the BIOS skip the memory test that occurs when you turn on your PC. It's a very basic test and the chances are, if you really do have bad memory, the test won't catch it anyway.

Note that some BIOSs have the Quick Power On Self Test enabled by default. Not all do though, so check it out.

Hot tip

While you have the Advanced BIOS Features page open, disable the Bootup Floppy Seek function as well. This will prevent the BIOS from attempting to detect and initialize the floppy drive during bootup, thus saving more time.

Unused Hardware

Every time a computer is switched on, its hardware has to be detected and initialized by the BIOS, as we saw on page 30. Thus, the more devices there are, the longer the PC takes to boot up.

While most of the PC's hardware is essential for it to run, in virtually all systems there are some devices that are not used. By disabling these, you can increase the PC's boot speed.

1 Go to Start, Control Panel, Device Manager. Here, you will see a list of all the hardware installed on your system

2 Go through the list (don't forget to expand the various categories) and disable any devices that you do not use. Do this by right-clicking the device and clicking Disable

Examples of devices that are typically unused include:

- Network adapters – most motherboards provide an integrated network adapter

- Modems – if you are using broadband, disable your dial-up modem (assuming you have one). Don't forget to check that there isn't one integrated on the motherboard

- Multimedia devices – for example, the author doesn't use the Game Port, so has disabled it on his machine

Beware

Do not attempt to disable hardware devices in the Display adapters and System categories. These are critical to the operation of your PC.

Hot tip

You may also find unused hardware that can be disabled in the BIOS. For example: parallel and serial ports, and integrated sound controllers.

32

Streamline the Fonts Folder

Windows 7 comes with a large number of fonts, all of which are installed in the Fonts folder. As each of these fonts are loaded when the PC starts up, the more there are the longer startup takes to complete. Therefore, you can increase your boot speed by deleting all but the ones used by the system, and the ones you yourself are likely to use.

1 Open the Windows folder on the hard drive and locate the Fonts folder. Right-click it, select Copy and save it in a backup location

2 Now open the original folder and simply work through the fonts, deleting any that you consider to be surplus to requirements; this should be the vast majority of them

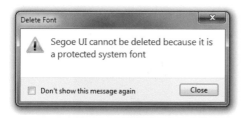

Note that some of the fonts are system fonts and are used by the operating system. If you try to delete any of these, you will see

the "cannot delete ..." message shown above.

Should you subsequently find a need for any of the deleted fonts, just copy them back to the Fonts folder from your backup folder.

Hot tip

A font manager can be very useful for users who access the fonts on their systems regularly. These can be downloaded from the Internet.

Beware

Be wary of downloading free fonts from the Internet. These are often corrupt and may cause your system to lock up completely.

Clear Out the Startup Folder

The next thing to look at is your startup programs. These are applications that open automatically when Windows starts and are located, you won't be surprised to learn, in the Startup folder.

Items can be placed here by the user if he or she wants them to open with Windows, so they are ready for immediate use. Also, some programs will automatically place a link here when they are installed.

As each of these programs must be loaded before Windows is ready for use, the more there are in the Startup folder, the longer it will take.

Check it out as follows:

Beware

The more programs you have in your Startup folder, the longer the PC will take to boot.

1 Click the Start button and then All Programs. Scroll down to Startup and open it

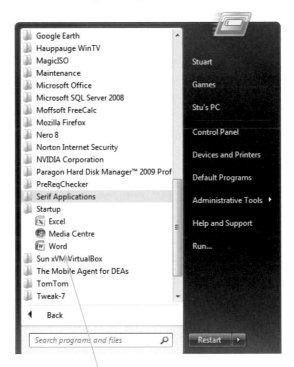

2 Here, you'll see a list of applications that start with Windows. Remove any that you don't need by right-clicking and clicking Delete

However, clearing out the Startup folder is only half the battle. You now have to find and get rid of the startup programs that run unseen in the background, and thus aren't so obvious.

1 Type msconfig in the Start Menu's search box and press Enter. This opens the System Configuration utility. Click the Startup tab

Hot tip

The System Configuration Utility is useful in more ways than one. Amongst other things, it allows you to view and stop the services running on your PC, troubleshoot boot problems, and launch various Windows tools.

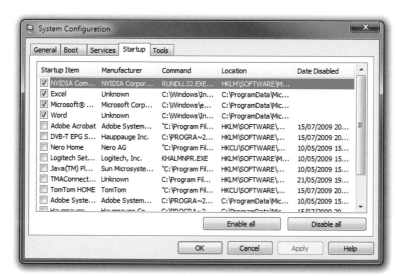

2 Here, you will see a list of more programs that start with Windows and it may come as something of a surprise

To disable a program, simply uncheck it. You can, in fact, quite safely disable all of them by clicking the Disable All button – none of them play any critical role (if they did, there wouldn't be a Disable All button).

However, we would suggest that you refrain from disabling your antivirus program, which will be listed here (assuming you have one) and Windows Defender. These applications both play an essential role in keeping your system free of viruses and malware.

Hot tip

If you want more information on any of the programs (it's not always obvious what they are or do), go to www.sysinfo.org. Here, you will find a huge list of applications that start with Windows, together with explanatory notes.

35

Screensavers and Wallpaper

In days gone by, computer monitors were prone to having an impression literally burnt into the screen by prolonged exposure to a static image. To guard against this unfortunate tendency, screensavers were invented. Quite apart from serving a useful purpose, they could also be fun.

These days however, that's all they are – fun. They are now completely superfluous in the modern computer system, as monitors are no longer susceptible to damage caused by static images.

Because a screensaver is actually a program, having one enabled means that Windows has one more application to load before it is ready to use. So reduce your PC's startup time by disabling any screensaver that is currently active. Do it by right-clicking the Desktop and clicking Personalize. Then click Screen Saver, and in the next dialog box select None from the drop-down box.

Beware

Be wary of using any of the 3D screensavers available on the Internet. Not only can they take a long time to load, they can also be buggy, and thus be the cause of system instability.

With regard to wallpaper, these are large image files that have no function other than to make your Desktop look snazzy. As with screensavers, they do slow down the startup procedure as they also have to be loaded by Windows.

Your best option here is to use a solid color as the background. Right-click the Desktop, select Personalize and then Desktop Background. From the drop-down box, select a color.

Boot Screen Blues

When Windows 7 is loading you will see an animated Windows logo open up, as shown below:

By telling Windows not to load this animation, the PC's bootup time can be reduced. Do it as follows:

1) Click the Start button
2) In the Search box, type msconfig
3 Press Enter

The System Configuration utility will now open. Click the Boot tab.

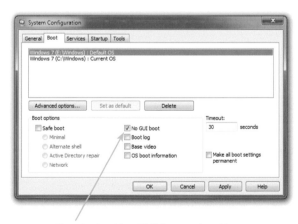

Check the No GUI boot checkbox

The next time you boot the PC, the animation will be bypassed.

Beware

The drawback with disabling the boot screen is that it does provide an indication when the PC's bootup is frozen.

Shutdown Issues

When a PC takes an unusually long time to shut down, the cause is almost always one of the following:

1)   A service, or running process, that is slow to close
2)   The unloading of user-profile files
3)   A non-responding application
4)   A corrupted or incompatible device driver

Hot tip

Shutdown issues can be difficult problems to identify. Device drivers are the most likely cause and this is what you should investigate first.

The first three in the list above have, to a certain degree, been addressed in Windows 7 and, therefore, do not cause as many problems as they did with previous versions of Windows. That said, on occasion, they are still the cause of shutdown issues.

Device drivers are beyond Windows' control as the decision of whether to install a particular driver is down to the user. Windows will warn the user if it thinks a driver being installed is potentially problematic but it cannot stop the installation. This is the biggest cause of shutdown problems with Windows (see pages 23-24 for how to eliminate driver issues).

When faced with a PC that takes its time to shut down, go to the Control Panel and open the Performance Information and Tools utility. Click Advanced Tools and then "View performance details in Event log".

Hot tip

The Event log will also highlight issues that are causing your PC to boot more slowly than it should.

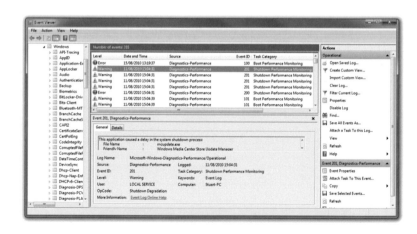

Look under the Task Category for issues relating to Shutdown Performance Monitoring. Clicking an entry will reveal details of the application that is causing a delay in the shutdown process. If you click the Event Log Online Help link, you will be taken to a Microsoft website where you may find more detailed information.

Kill Services Quickly

When a PC's Shutdown button is pressed, Windows closes all open applications, including any services that may be running. The length of time Windows allocates for the latter is set by the WaitToKillServiceTimeout registry key; the default setting of which is 12000 ms (12 seconds).

If all running services stop within 12 seconds, the PC shuts down. However, if they don't, the user is presented with a dialog box, which offers two options: wait for the service to stop of its own accord or force it to close.

By amending the default value, it is possible to automatically force tardy services to close more quickly and thus prevent them from slowing down the shutdown procedure.

In the Start Menu search box, type regedit and press Enter. Windows Registry Editor will open. Navigate to the following key:

HKEY_Local_Machine/System/CurrentControlSet/Control

Click the Control folder on the left and then on the right you will see the WaitToKillServiceTimeout key.

Beware

Resist the temptation to set too low a value as this may lead to loss of data. Applications do need some time to close. The object here is simply to speed the process up somewhat. A figure of 5000 to 6000 ms will be about right.

39

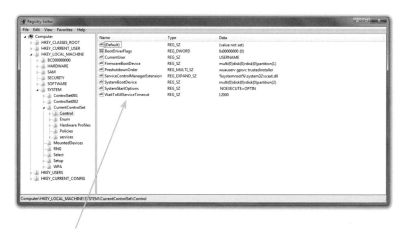

Double-click the key and in the Edit String dialog box that opens, enter a lower value.

No More Shutdown Woes

Windows 7 provides an option for closing down your machine known as "Sleep". This is accessible on the Start menu as shown below:

Hot tip

On laptops, Sleep mode only saves an image to the memory – not to the hard drive as well. It then monitors the battery and if it runs low, transfers the image stored in the memory to the hard drive.

The Sleep power mode is basically a combination of the Hibernate mode and the old Standby power mode.

In Hibernate mode, an image of the system is created on the hard drive and then the PC is powered off. The problem is that, in practice, it is not much quicker than just switching off and then back on as normal.

In the old Standby mode (not available in Windows 7), an image of the system was created in memory and power was maintained only to essential devices such as the CPU. The problem here was that an application could override Standby and keep the PC running. Also, if power to the PC was lost for some reason, e.g. a power blackout, all unsaved data was also lost.

Windows 7's Sleep mode saves all data in use to both the memory *and* the hard drive before cutting power to all but a few key components. The procedure takes about ten seconds. When a key is pressed or the mouse is moved, the system is restored from the image stored in the memory. If the machine has been powered off, the system is restored from the image stored on the hard drive. Thus, there is no danger of data loss.

Furthermore, and this is the major advantage of Sleep, it is quick, taking approximately three seconds to bring the PC back to life.

Sleep mode eliminates the need to switch a computer off between sessions at all. Simply put the machine to sleep at the end of the day, and then have it up-and-running within three seconds the following morning with a single keystroke or mouse click.

3 Productivity

Computers can be used for both entertainment and work. In this chapter we focus on the latter, looking at ways to increase the efficiency with which you use the PC. These will help you to save time, and also be more productive.

Find it Fast

A very important aspect of working efficiently and productively, is being able to locate things quickly when you need them. The workman who can lay his hand on the right tool as and when needed will get the job done faster than the one who always has to hunt about for it.

Working on a PC is no different so, to make life easier for users in this respect, Windows 7 provides a Search utility. This is tightly integrated in the operating system and thus, is instantly accessible from virtually any location. You will find it on the Start Menu (the search box at the bottom) and in any Explorer folder.

One of its best features is that it is contextual, i.e. its search is based on the user's current activity, whether it's searching for utilities in the Control Panel, for music files in Windows Media Player, or for files and applications in the Start Menu.

When doing a search, you have two ways to go:

Folder Searches

If you already know which folder the file is located in, use the search box at the top-right of the folder. By default, the search will be restricted to the contents of the folder, including any sub-folders.

You can also use filters to speed up the search. You will see these appear under the search box when you click in it. These enable you to search by date (exact or approximate), and by size.

Alternatively, near the top of the folder window, you will see options for searching in Libraries, Homegroups, Computer, Custom and Internet. For example, if you click Computer, the entire PC will be searched. The Custom option allows you to specify a specific location within the PC.

42

Don't forget

By default, a folder search will only find content that is located in the folder the search is conducted from.

Hot tip

Having done a search, you also have the option to save it for future reference. The Save button appears on the folder's menu bar when the search is finished.

To access the search at a later date, click your personal folder (the top-right item on the Start Menu) and then click the Search folder.

System Searches

If you have no idea where a file is located, and no information that will help in finding it, use the Start Menu search box. This will search the entire computer and will be your quickest option.

With this option you can locate not only files and folders, but also programs, emails and offline web pages.

Search Aids

Windows 7 provides two very useful tools that enable the user to increase the efficiency with which the Search utility is used.

File Indexer

The first is the Indexing utility. When the operating system is run for the first time, it creates an index of all the files in the most commonly used locations (not the entire computer, note). As a result, subsequent searches are much faster as Windows searches the index rather than the computer.

However, users who are in the habit of scattering files all over the place, or add storage devices to the PC, e.g. a second hard drive, can configure the utility to index any location they wish, or even the entire system.

To do this, go to Start, Control Panel, Indexing Options. Click Modify and then select the locations to be indexed.

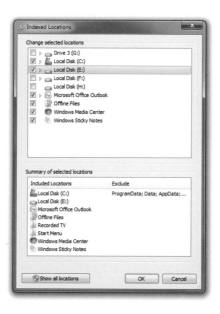

Don't forget

If you have any information regarding a file you're looking for, using it in conjunction with search filters will enable the file to be located more quickly.

Beware

If you decide to index the entire computer, be aware that the procedure can take several hours. During this time, system performance may be adversely affected. This only needs to be done once though, so it's not a major deal.

Tags

Tags provide a method of invisibly marking selected files. This makes the procedure of subsequently finding and organizing them much quicker and more efficient.

Don't forget

Tags provide a very useful means of not just locating data but also organizing it.

To use this feature, open the folder containing the file to be tagged, select it, and then go to the Details pane at the bottom of the window.

Don't forget

The Tag feature is not available for all file types. Microsoft file types, e.g. .doc (Word), and image files can be tagged but files from many third-party applications can't.

Click Add a Tag and enter an appropriate word or phrase. Then click Save.

As an example of how to use Tags, the author has used the word "book" to tag all the documents and images used in this book as he is not particularly well organized and leaves stuff all over the place. By doing a search for Book, on several occasions he has been able to locate all relevant files immediately.

More Right-Click Options

The right-click menu offers many useful options. Let's see how to add some more:

Move To Folder and Copy To Folder

The right-click Cut and Copy commands allow you to copy and move files to different locations. However, you have to go to the desired location to complete the operation. Here's a faster way.

1 Open the Registry Editor and locate the following key:
HKEY_CLASSES_ROOT\AllFilesystemObjects\
shellex\ContextMenuHandlers

Hot tip

Both of these commands also enable you to quickly create a new folder in the desired location without having to leave the dialog box.

2 Right-click the ContextMenuHandlers folder and select New, Key. Name the key Copy To. Double-click the default value in the right-hand window and enter the following in the Value Data box:
{C2FBB630-2971-11D1-A18C-00C04FD75D13}

3 Repeat the above procedure, this time naming the key Move To. In the Value Data box enter the following:
{C2FBB631-2971-11D1-A18C-00C04FD75D13}

Close the Registry Editor. Now right-click a folder or file and you will see Copy To Folder, and Move To Folder options.

These commands provide a very useful means of quickly relocating data without having to go to the actual location.

You don't need to reboot to make this change effective.

...cont'd

Add Options to the Send To Menu

The Send To menu provides another very useful method of quickly relocating data. It can also be used to open a file with an application the file is not associated with. For example, if your image files open with Windows Photo Viewer, you can use the Send To feature to open an image with a different image viewer.

If an application you would like to use in this way is not in the default Send To list, you can add it as described below:

1 The SendTo folder is hidden by default. To reveal it, open Folder Options in the Control Panel and click the View tab. Then select "Show hidden files and folders"

2 Click your user-name on the Start menu and then click AppData, Roaming, Microsoft, Windows. Now, you will see the SendTo folder

3 In the SendTo folder, create shortcuts to the applications you want to add to the Send To menu

4 When you have finished, close the folder and return to the Desktop. Your applications will now be available from the Send To menu

Hot tip

While the majority of programs work with the Send To feature, not all do. So if you try this and the program doesn't appear in the Send To list, don't waste time trying to figure out why. An example is programs from Microsoft Office Suites, such as Word, Excel and Frontpage.

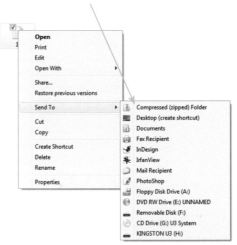

In this example, we have added Send To options for InDesign, PhotoShop and IrfanView.

Quick File Selection

The traditional way of selecting a bunch of files is to drag a box around them with the left mouse button depressed. Individual files are selected by holding down the Ctrl key.

Windows 7 provides a better way:

1 Open any folder and click Tools on the menu bar. Click Folder Options and then the View tab

Hot tip

To deselect a number of check box selected files, left-click once in an empty part of the folder.

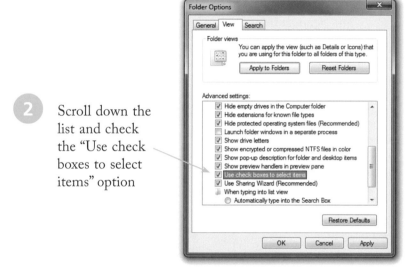

2 Scroll down the list and check the "Use check boxes to select items" option

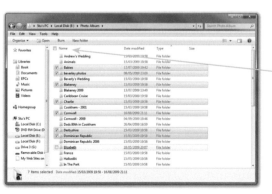

The next time you open a folder, you will see a check box at the top of the window next to Name. Checking this will automatically select every file

Hot tip

You can still select files in the traditional way by dragging a box round them.

in the folder. If you want to select individual files, hovering the mouse over the file will open a check box to the left of the file, as shown above. Simply check the box to select the file.

This method is quicker and more precise.

Computing on the Move

We saw on page 10 that a flash drive can be used to improve the performance of a PC courtesy of the ReadyBoost feature. Well, here's another extremely useful way to use one of these devices.

You will need a flash drive that is supplied with U3 Smart Management software (if yours isn't, you can download it from www.u3.com). This software enables you to install programs directly to the flash drive. Once done, you can then plug the drive into a different PC and run the programs without having to install them on that PC. You can also run them on your own PC.

The possible uses for this are endless. For example, if you want to show some friends a video and know they don't have a suitable media player on their PC, you can play the video from a media player installed on the flash drive.

The first step is to install the U3 software. Then you will see a new icon in the Notification Area.

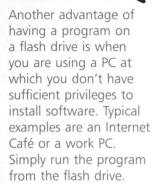

Hot tip

Another advantage of having a program on a flash drive is when you are using a PC at which you don't have sufficient privileges to install software. Typical examples are an Internet Café or a work PC. Simply run the program from the flash drive.

Clicking it will bring up the Launchpad (shown left) from where you can run programs, explore the drive, change settings, etc.

At the bottom, you will see a Download Programs button. Clicking this takes you to www.u3.com; here you can download and automatically install more programs.

Hot tip

Useful U3 compatible applications include:

- OpenOffice (fully featured office suite)
- Mozilla Firefox web browser
- Skype (Internet phone calls)

Note that it is only possible to install software that has been adapted for U3 – you can't install just any program. However, the list of available software is comprehensive and includes the most commonly used types of application – media players, office suites, utilities, etc. (see margin note). Furthermore, the U3 project is rapidly growing in popularity and so the list is expanding fast.

Batch Renaming of Files

Have you ever been in a situation in which you have a bunch of related files with an assortment of meaningless or unrelated names? To make order of them, you have to individually rename each file, which can be a tedious task.

Well, all that is now a thing of the past. Windows 7 provides you with a means of sequentially renaming any number of files with the minimum of effort.

1 Select the files to be renamed

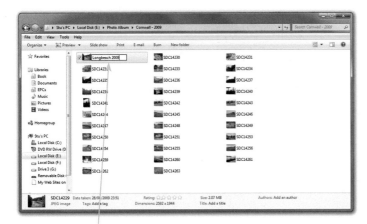

2 Right-click the first file in the list and click Rename. Type in a suitable name and then click anywhere in the folder. The files will now all be automatically renamed, as shown below

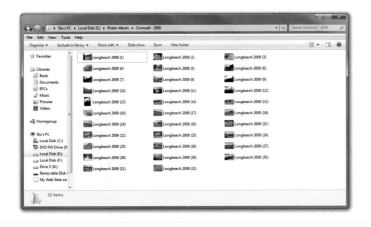

Hot tip

Use the Windows check box feature to select your files as described on page 47.

Hot tip

Should you want to revert to the original file names, reselect the files, click the Organize button and then click Undo.

Change/Set File Associations

All files are designed to be opened with a specific type of program. For example, graphics files, such as JPEG and GIF, can only be opened by a graphics editing program, e.g. Paint, or with a web browser, such as Internet Explorer.

A common problem that many users experience is when they install a program on their PC that automatically makes itself the default program for opening related files. If the user prefers the original program, he or she will have to reassociate the file type in question. Alternatively, the user might want to set a different program as the default.

Don't forget

If a newly installed program has rudely hijacked your favorite files, you can send it to the doghouse by reassociating the file with your favored program.

1 Go to Start, Control Panel, Default Programs. Click "Associate a file type or protocol with a program"

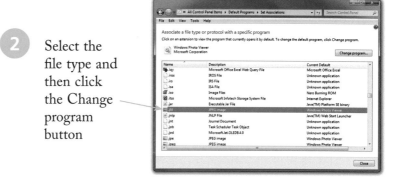

2 Select the file type and then click the Change program button

Hot tip

Another way is to right-click a file and then click Properties. Click the General tab and then click Change. Browse to the program you want to open the file with and select it.

3 If the desired program is in the list, select it and click OK. If it isn't, click Browse and locate it manually

Close Non-Responding Programs

Every computer user has experienced this. You close a program but instead of disappearing gracefully and without fuss, it insists on hanging around. You click the red X button repeatedly but it refuses to go.

When this happens, after a few moments a dialog box will open asking if you want to wait until the program closes or whether you want to close it yourself. The latter option will usually do the trick; however, it doesn't always work.

In this situation, do the following:

1 Right-click the Taskbar and click Task Manager

2 Click the Applications tab and you will see the non-responding program. Select it and then click the End Task button

3 If even this doesn't work, right-click the program and click Go To Process. Then click the End Process button

Beware

If you haven't already saved your data, closing a non-responding application with the Task Manager may result in you losing that data.

51

Hot tip

Every now and again, you will open a web page that causes your browser to stop responding. Use this tip to close it.

Create Your Own Toolbars

Most people create shortcuts on the Desktop for frequently used programs, thus enabling them to be accessed quickly. The problem with this is that you can end up with a Desktop cluttered with loads of icons. Here's another way:

1 Create a folder on the Desktop and place shortcuts to the required applications in the folder. Give it a suitable name and then close it

Don't forget

Creating toolbars provides a useful means of quickly accessing your applications, and also keeping the Desktop free of clutter.

2 Right-click the Taskbar and select Toolbars, New Toolbar

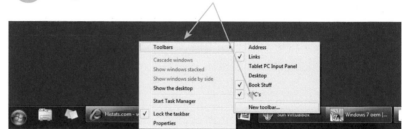

3 Browse to the newly created folder and click Select Folder

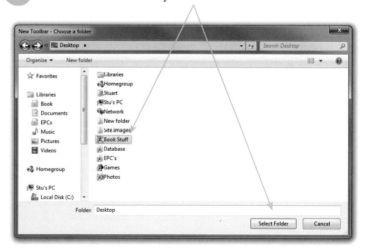

 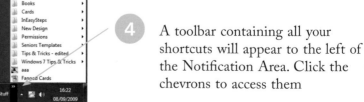

4 A toolbar containing all your shortcuts will appear to the left of the Notification Area. Click the chevrons to access them

Create a Customized Control Panel

The Control Panel is a very useful and often overlooked section of the operating system. From here, you can access settings that affect virtually all aspects of the computer.

It does, however, contain quite a few applications that will be of no interest to the average user: Sync Center, Credential Manager, and Speech Recognition, are typical examples. There are others though, such as Internet Options, System, and Administrative Tools, that many people will use frequently.

This tip will give you quick access to the ones you use and allow you to forget about the ones you don't use.

1 Create a new folder on the Desktop and name it Control Panel

2 Open the Control Panel (the real one) and create Desktop shortcuts to the applications you use (right-click and select Create Shortcut)

3 Close the Control Panel and go back to the Desktop. Now drag the shortcuts to the Control Panel folder

Hot tip

Take some time to look through the Control Panel utilities. You will discover a lot of Windows features that you didn't know existed, plus, you will learn a lot about your computer.

Hot tip

You can also use your new Control Panel folder to create a toolbar on the Taskbar as described on page 52.

You will now have a Control Panel on the Desktop that contains only the applications that you use. This will enable you to locate the items quickly instead of having to search through a long list.

Organize Your Data

Windows 7 includes a new feature known as Libraries. This is basically a data management system that enables the user to quickly and easily organize specific types of data, e.g. images, documents, videos, etc.

The concept behind this is that of a single folder known as a Library, which contains user-defined subfolders. The subfolders are not actually stored in the library though; they are still in their original locations. These could be a different hard drive, a flash drive or even a separate PC (in the case of a networked system). However, they are all instantly accessible from the library folder. Furthermore, any changes to the contents of the subfolders, wherever they may be, are dynamically updated in the library.

Windows 7 starts you off with four default libraries: Music, Documents, Pictures and Videos, which cover the main file types. These can be accessed by left-clicking the Windows Explorer icon on the left-hand side of the Taskbar.

However, should you wish to create a new library, you can do so by clicking New library on the menu bar. Then open your new library by clicking its icon and then click "Include a folder" to add content to it. To add further folders to the library, you then need to click location under the library's name.

Hot tip

If you simply like things neat and tidy, or have a genuine need to organize your data efficiently, Windows 7's Libraries feature is just what you need.

Hot tip

Windows indexes all library folders to enable fast searching.

Used in conjunction, Windows Tags feature (see page 44), and Llibraries provide a quick method of assimilating data and then efficiently organizing it into easily accessible locations.

Windows XP Mode (XPM)

Windows XP Mode is a new feature to Windows. It provides a virtual PC platform from which a pre-activated edition of Windows XP Professional Service Pack 3 can be run within the Windows 7 environment. Basically, it's a PC within a PC. Everything you can do on a real PC, such as printing and browsing the Internet, can also be done on the virtual PC.

The purpose is two-fold: First, there are many users who will still rather have XP as their main system but would also like to have Windows 7 with its new features and capabilities. Second, many users are still using programs that run fine on XP but not on Windows 7. XPM enables both types of user to have the best of both worlds – XP as their main system or to run legacy software, and also have Windows 7.

XPM works in two ways:

1) You can run the virtual XP PC as Windows XP, i.e, from a Windows XP Desktop

2) You can run programs installed on the virtual XP PC from Windows 7, i.e, from a Windows 7 Desktop

Applications installed on the XP machine will also be accessible on Windows 7 and vice versa. XP applications started from the Windows 7 All Programs list will appear to be running on Windows 7.

However, XPM is not built-in to Windows 7. The application has to be downloaded from the Microsoft website, and consists of a modified version of Microsoft's Virtual PC application and an activated image file of Windows XP.

First you install Virtual PC and then the image of Windows XP. Having done so, under All Programs in Windows 7's Start Menu you will see a new entry – Windows Virtual PC. Open this and you will see two items.

The first – Virtual Machines, you can ignore. The second – Virtual Windows XP, opens a Windows XP virtual PC on your Windows 7 Desktop as shown on the next page.

Hot tip

You can only use XPM if your PC is capable of hardware virtualization. Intel and AMD both provide a utility that will check your PC for this capability. These can be downloaded from their websites. This should only be necessary with older PCs, though – modern systems will already have it.

...cont'd

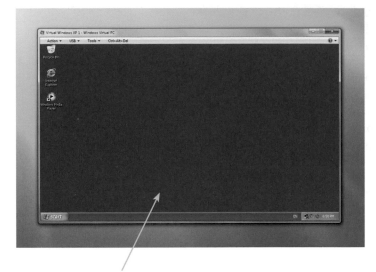

Don't forget

When you use a virtual XP PC, it will seem that you are actually running Windows 7. However, if you want the look of XP, you can change the default setting to show an XP Desktop, as shown on the right.

Windows XP Desktop running on a Windows 7 PC

The final step is to install the applications you want to run on your XP virtual PC. Having done so, if you now go back to the Windows 7 All Programs menu and click Windows Virtual PC, you will see an entry called Virtual Windows XP Applications. Open this and the applications you have installed (Microsoft Office in the example below) on the virtual PC, will be listed.

Hot tip

Files created on an XP virtual PC can be saved and accessed on the Windows 7 PC, and vice versa.

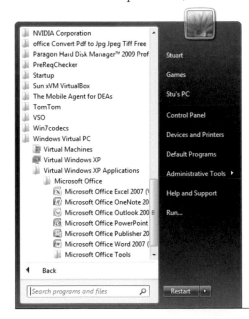

If you run any of them from here, the program will open on the Windows 7 Desktop as though it were installed on Windows 7. It will, however, actually be running on the XP virtual machine.

All your PC's drives and peripheral hardware will be accessible to the XP virtual PC.

Windows Explorer Internet Search

Windows 7 introduces an advanced search facility called Federated Search, which allows you to search the Internet, or a specific website, from within Windows Explorer.

It works by installing what's known as a search connector on your PC. These are small .osdx text files that you either download and install on your PC, or create yourself. There are many of these connectors readily available on the Internet for sites such as Flickr, YouTube, Twitter, Amazon and eBay, etc.

To install a search connector, simply click the icon and the following dialog box will appear:

Click Add to install the connector

Open any Explorer window and you will see installed connectors in the Favorites list on the left

Hot tip

You will still need a browser to view the results of a search connector search. However, you can see a preview of the search result by enabling the preview pane of the window you are working in.

Click a connector and then in the Search box at the top-right of the window, type your query. The results will appear automatically

Miscellaneous Tips

Access an Inaccessible PC
Some programs run in full-screen mode when they are installed, thus hiding both the Desktop and Taskbar. Also, many games do the same by running permanently in full-screen mode.

If you need to open a file or program when in this situation, you can access the PC by pressing the Windows key (this has a logo of a flying window printed on it). This opens the Start Menu; from there you can get into the PC.

Switch to Full-Screen Mode
When you're working in a folder that contains a large amount of files, you can reduce the amount of scrolling necessary by simply pressing the F11 key. This switches the folder to full-screen view. Press F11 again to revert to the normal view.

Restore Previous Folders at Logon
If you log off with a bunch of folders open, Windows closes them all for you. If you want the folders to reopen in their original size and position when you log on again, do the following:

Hot tip

If you want to rename a file, rather than right-clicking it and clicking Rename, select it with the mouse and then press F2.

Hot tip

Have you ever needed to insert the date and time in a notepad document? Here's an easy way: rather than typing it, just press the F5 key.

1 Open any folder, click Tools, Folder Options and then the View tab

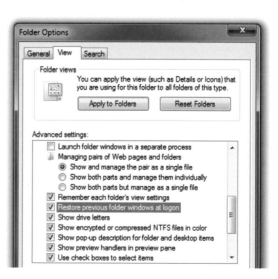

2 Check the "Restore previous folder windows at logon" box

Bypass the Recycle Bin

If you can live without the safety net provided by the Recycle Bin, you can speed up file deletion by doing away with it completely.

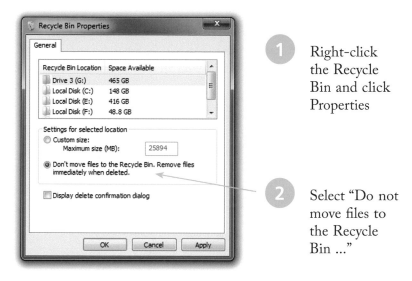

1 Right-click the Recycle Bin and click Properties

2 Select "Do not move files to the Recycle Bin ..."

Hot tip

Another way to bypass the Recycle Bin is to hold down the Shift key as you click Delete.

Start Your Favorite Programs Automatically

This tip will enable you to start any application automatically with Windows, so it is up and running when the Desktop appears.

1 Go to Start, All Programs. Right-click the Startup folder and click Open

2 Create shortcuts to the programs you want to auto-start in the Startup folder

The next time you start the PC the programs will launch automatically.

Quick Zoom

If you want to zoom in on the contents of a folder (one containing photos, for example), instead of using the Views menu, hold down the Ctrl key and scroll the mouse wheel. Move forward to zoom in and backwards to zoom out. This works in any Windows folder, on the Desktop, Internet Explorer and most third-party applications.

Hot tip

When working in Windows, a quick way to undo your last action is to press Ctrl+Z. For example: you have deleted a file by mistake. Rather than opening the Recycle Bin and searching through it, pressing Ctrl+Z will restore the file instantly.

Quick Search

You've got a text document open and need to find a specific word, or all instances of one. The Windows Search utility isn't much use in this situation.

Rather than read laboriously through the document, just press Ctrl+F. This opens a Find utility that will go straight to the required word and highlight it for you.

Hot tip

Internet Explorer has a similar feature called Copy Shortcut. This is also available from the right-click menu and lets you copy and paste a link as text. Very handy for inserting a link in an email, for example.

If you need to find another instance of the word, click the Find Next button

This works in any Windows text document, such as Notepad, Wordpad and Journal. It also works in most word-processors and desktop publishing applications.

Copy as Path

Here's a handy little feature that can be a real time saver. Now and again, you need to find out the exact path of a file or folder. This could be to change a setting in the registry, or to copy a link from a network file share into an email, etc.

The usual way of doing this is to right-click the file and click Properties. Next to Location in the General tab, you will find the file's path. Then you copy and paste it.

A much quicker way is to simply right-click the file or folder while holding the Shift key down, and click Copy as Path. Then go to your email or whatever, right-click and click Paste. Voila! Job done.

4 Things You Can Do Without

This chapter shows you how to get rid of some of the more irritating features found in Windows 7.

User Account Control (UAC)

User Account Control is a security feature designed to protect users from themselves, i.e. unwittingly making changes to the system that can compromise its security.

The most obvious manifestations of UAC are the "Do you want to allow ..." dialog boxes that pop up when the user tries to do certain actions – installing a program, for example – and the Secure Desktop (when access to the Desktop is removed).

These quickly become extremely tiresome, so getting rid of UAC (or reducing its level) is probably the first thing most users will want to do. This is actually very simple as we see below:

1 Go to Start, Control Pancl, User Accounts. Click "Change User Account Control settings"

2 Drag the slider to adjust the level of UAC (bottom is off completely)

Beware

You should not disable UAC completely unless you are aware of the security issues involved. It is there for a reason.

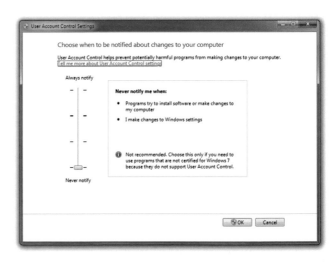

Puncture Balloon Tips

Many people find the balloon tips that regularly spring up from the Notification Area very irritating. Although they do sometimes give useful information, much of the time it is something obvious or that is already known to the user.

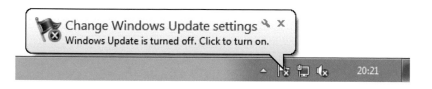

For those of you who can do without these tips, the solution is as follows:

1 Go to Start, Control Panel, Action Center

2 Click "Change Action Center settings"

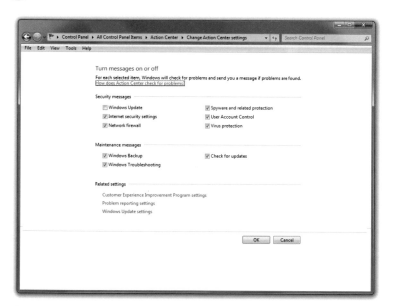

3 Remove the check marks from the notifications you don't want to receive

Balloon tips do come up with something worth knowing sometimes. For example, if your hard drive is running low on space, a balloon will pop up advising you of the fact. So you disable them at your own risk. Our recommendation is to leave them enabled.

Goodbye to Problem Reports

Every time an application experiences an error and is closed down by the system, Windows Problem Reporting utility will spring to life asking if you want to send details about the problem to Microsoft.

If you're the one in a million who will actually do this, then read no further. If you've no intention of complying though, you'll want to get rid of this irritation as soon as possible.

Don't forget

Before you disable Problem Reports, you should be aware that if it is available, Microsoft will send you the solution to the problem. So while it is undoubtedly irritating, it can help you to prevent a repeat occurrence of the issue.

1 Go to Start, Control Panel and click Administrative Tools. Then click Services

2 In the dialog box that opens, scroll down to Windows Error Reporting Service and in the drop-down box next to Startup type, select Disabled

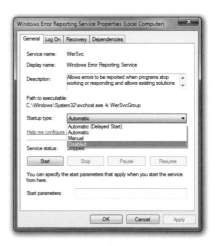

Aero Peek

Another new feature in Windows 7 is Aero Peek. This will reveal the Desktop when the cursor is placed over the Show Desktop button:

Aero Peek button

It does this by hiding any open windows and instead showing the outline of where they were. While this is pretty cool, it can be annoying when the cursor is moved accidentally to the button and thus hides the window you are working in.

So you can disable this feature by doing the following:

1 Right-click an empty area of the Taskbar and click Properties

2 Remove the check from the "Use Aero Peek to preview the desktop" checkbox

Aero Snap

Windows 7 features a novel new way to arrange your windows. This is known as Aero Snap and basically it provides a quick way of resizing and tiling windows.

However, like Aero Peek, this is a feature that many users will want to disable, as at times it will cause you to resize a window when all you were intending to do was move it to a different part of the screen.

Aero Snap can be disabled as follows:

1 Go to Start, Control Panel, Ease of Access Center

2 Click "make the mouse easier to use"

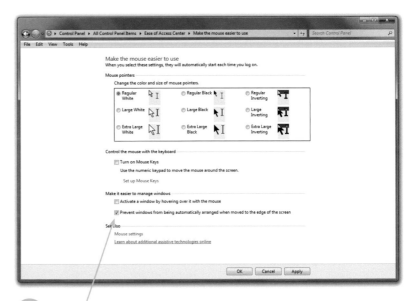

3 Check the "Prevent windows from being automatically arranged when moved to the edge of the screen" checkbox

Hot tip

The premise behind Aero Snap is to simplify the process of dragging & dropping between two windows, or comparing their content. Previously, this involved resizing and suitably positioning the two windows, which can take a considerable amount of mouse movement.

With Aero Snap, you can grab a window and move your mouse to the edge of the screen and the window will resize to fill half the screen. Repeat with the other window. Now with two motions you have a setup that makes both of these scenarios much easier to accomplish.

Unwanted Windows Features

With Windows 7, Microsoft have made an effort to streamline the operating system by not including applications that have been standard in previous versions. For example: Windows Messenger, Windows Mail, Movie Maker, etc. With some new applications such as Windows XP Mode, it is up to the user whether or not to download and install them. Programs and features that many users may never use are no longer being forced on them.

There is also a way to further streamline Windows and you can do it as described below:

1 In the Start Menu search box, type "windows features". You will see the following:

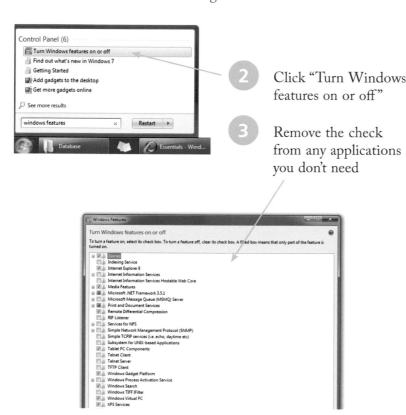

2 Click "Turn Windows features on or off"

3 Remove the check from any applications you don't need

Hot tip

Deselecting a feature doesn't mean that you are uninstalling it. What happens is that the next time the PC is started, Windows won't load the files necessary for the feature to work. Re-select it and it will be available after you next reboot your system.

As a typical example, if you use the superior Firefox web browser, you can disable Internet Explorer 8. With previous versions of Windows, there was no way to do this.

AutoPlay

AutoPlay is one of those Windows features that attempts to be helpful by providing related options that the user may not know how to access. Whenever removable media (DVDs, external hard drive, USB flash drive), etc., is connected to the PC, a dialog box opens offering options that Windows thinks is relevant to the content on the media.

Experienced Windows users, however, have no need for AutoPlay and find it is more of a nuisance than anything else. It can be disabled, or modified, as follows:

Hot tip

AutoPlay has long been regarded as an unsecure feature that provides an entry point for viruses. The version supplied with Windows 7 is much more secure.

 Go to Start, Control Panel and open AutoPlay

 To disable AutoPlay completely, uncheck "Use AutoPlay for all media and devices"

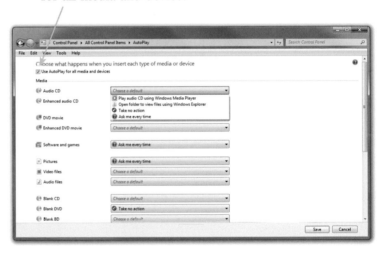

If you find the feature useful for certain types of media, you can modify the way AutoPlay behaves when media of that type is connected to the PC.

Just click the relevant drop-down box and choose a suitable option from the ones shown.

5 Customization

There are many ways
to change the default
appearance of Windows 7 in
order to personalize the PC.
This chapter shows you the
most common ones, plus
some others that are
not so well known.

The Windows Interface

Customizing the appearance of Windows allows you to create an environment that you feel comfortable in. Your first decision will be which of Windows 7's interfaces to use – Aero, Windows 7 Basic or Windows Classic.

Aero

When you run Windows 7 for the first time, the Aero interface may, or may not, be enabled by default – see top margin note.

If it is, you'll notice immediately the translucent effect that is applied to Window borders. This is one of the first things that you may want to alter to your own tastes.

1 Right-click an empty area of the Desktop and click Personalize. This opens the Personalization utility

2 Click Window Color at the bottom of the dialog box

3 Choose from a range of preset options

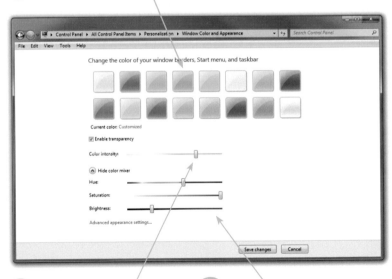

4 Adjust the level of color intensity

5 If you don't like any of the presets, use the color mixer to get the exact effect you want

Hot tip

If your hardware is capable of supporting the Aero interface it will be enabled by default. If it isn't, the interface will be Windows 7 Basic.

Hot tip

Choose Aero if you want the fancy graphic effects, such as transparency, glowing maximize and minimize buttons, Taskbar thumbnails and Flip 3D.

Windows 7 Basic

If you don't like Aero or your system is struggling to cope with it, try a different option:

1 In the Personalization utility, scroll down to the bottom of the dialog box

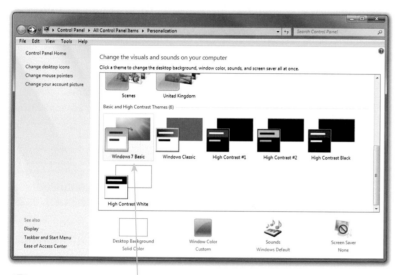

Don't forget

If good performance is your criteria, then Windows 7 Basic is the better option. You will lose the eye-catching graphics but will have a faster PC.

2 Select Windows 7 Basic

With Windows 7 Basic, you will lose the translucent window borders and Aero's graphics effects, such as Taskbar icon thumbnails (shown below), and shadows. In its place, you get a solid light blue window border.

Don't forget

Don't forget about the Windows Classic interface. This is clean, simple and fast, which is why many power users still prefer it.

You will, however, lose none of the operating system's functionality.

The Desktop

The next thing to customize is the Desktop. Here, you have four things to look at:

Size (Resolution)

The first is the Desktop's resolution. If it's too high, the Desktop will be too small, i.e. it won't stretch to the full width and depth of the monitor, plus the icons and icon text will be tiny. If it's too low, the Desktop will be too big and everything will be chunky and blocky.

The recommended settings are:

- 17- and 19-inch monitors – 1280 x 1024
- 20- and 21-inch monitors – 1600 x 1200
- 23-inch monitors – 1920 x 1200

Check this out as follows:

1   Right-click the Desktop and click Screen Resolution

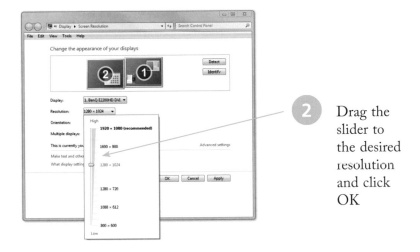

2   Drag the slider to the desired resolution and click OK

Hot tip

While you have the Screen Resolution dialog box open, check that your refresh rate is correct. Click Advanced Settings and then the Monitor tab. Under Screen Refresh Rate, select the highest setting available from the drop-down box.

Icon Size

If you don't like the default size of the Desktop icons, there are two ways to change it:

1)   Right-click the Desktop and select View. Then choose from three preset options: large, medium or small

2)   Hold down the Ctrl key and scroll the mouse wheel. This will enable you to set the icon size exactly

Wallpaper

Now turn your attention to the wallpaper – it's a fair bet that you won't want to keep the default image. Select your own by right-clicking the Desktop and clicking Personalize. Then click Desktop Background.

Make your selection and click Save Changes

Icon Text

The final thing you may want to change is the size of the icon text.

1 Right-click the Desktop and click Personalize. Then click Display and then "Set custom text size (DPI)" at the left. In the DPI Scaling dialog box, click "Custom DPI..."

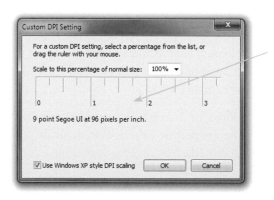

2 Hold the pointer over the ruler and drag to adjust the font size

Hot tip

If you don't like any of Windows wallpapers, it's a simple matter to make your own. All you need to know is where to put them.

Windows Wallpaper folder is located in the Windows folder on the hard drive. Open it and scroll down to the Web folder. Inside this is the Wallpaper folder. Place your images here and Windows will automatically resize them when they are selected.

Hot tip

Following on from the tip above, be aware that image proportions should be similar to those of Windows wallpapers (4 x 3). Otherwise, some of it will be cropped out during the resizing.

73

Create Your Own Theme

Getting Windows looking just like you want it can take some time. Unfortunately, if you, or somebody else, subsequently change it again you'll never be able to recreate it exactly as it was.

There is, however, an easy way round this. Windows allows you to save your theme settings so you can get them back with a single mouse click.

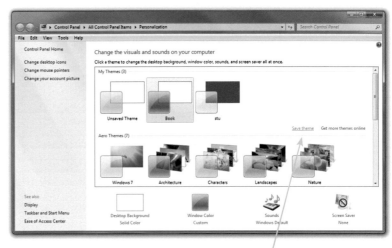

Hot tip

To create a shared theme, simply right-click a theme and then click "Save theme for sharing". The theme will be saved with a .themepack file format that can be applied on another computer running Windows 7.

1 Having created your theme, click "Save theme"

2 Give your theme a name

At the top of the Personalization utility window, under My Themes, your new theme will be listed. Just click to select it. You can create and save any number of themes.

Another option provided by Windows 7 enables you to share the themes you create, or use those created by others. For example, a theme can be uploaded to a website from where it can be downloaded by other users. Or you can save it on removable media and load it on to another PC.

Get More Windows Themes

Windows 7 doesn't provide much in the way of themes and, what little there is, is essentially just variations of the same basic theme.

If you want more, your only option is to fire-up your browser and head off into cyberspace. Here, you will discover that there is a virtually limitless amount of themes, or "Skins" as they are often called, available for download.

These come in an infinite range of colors and styles and will enable you to radically change the way Windows looks. The illustrations below show two (rather extreme) examples:

75

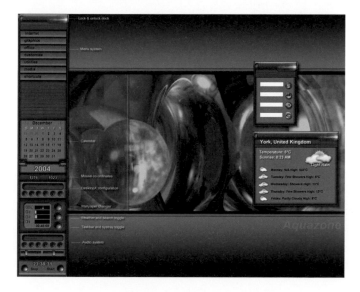

Hot tip

If you're interested in themes, visit www. wincustomize.com. Here, you will find hundreds of categorized themes for Windows, all available for free download.

Beware

Some of the themes available on the Internet can be buggy and thus, cause instability problems on the PC.

The Taskbar

The Taskbar is a highly configurable part of Windows and setting it up to suit your method of working is important. There are quite a few adjustments you can make here that are not obvious at first glance.

Taskbar Size and Position

The first thing you might want to change is the size of the Taskbar. The default setting is quite narrow and looks like this:

By right-clicking the Taskbar and selecting Properties, you will see that the small icons option is selected by default. Deselect this to increase the depth of the Taskbar, as shown below:

You can also resize the Taskbar to any depth you require by right-clicking and de-selecting "Lock the taskbar". Then hold the cursor over the top edge of the Taskbar and you will be able to drag it to the size you want. Then relock it. However, this can look a bit odd as the icons are placed at the top, as shown below:

You can get round this by docking the Taskbar at the right or left of the screen. Here, we see it docked at the right.

Hot tip

If you want to change the order of a Taskbar icon, simply drag it to the required position. This also applies to icons in the Notification area.

Hot tip

Right-clicking a Taskbar icon reveals a jump list of recent files associated with the application. You can also access the jump list by left-clicking an icon and dragging upwards at the same time.

Do this by unlocking it as previously described and simply dragging it to the required location. Increasing the Taskbar's width and having it docked at the side of the screen is an ideal way of making use of the extra screen real estate provided by modern wide-screen monitors.

If you need as much screen space as possible, you can also auto-hide the Taskbar so that it releases the space it occupies when not being accessed.

Do this by right-clicking the Taskbar and selecting Properties. Then uncheck "Auto-hide the taskbar".

Hot tip

In Windows 7, the old Quick Launch toolbar has disappeared. However, you can get it back by right-clicking the Taskbar, selecting Toolbars, New toolbar and then typing the following: %userprofile%\AppData\Roaming\Microsoft\Internet Explorer\Quick Launch.
  Then click Select Folder and the Quick Launch toolbar will appear on the Taskbar.

While you have the Taskbar and Start Menu Properties dialog box open, you can also set how icons are displayed on the Taskbar. The default is grouped, whereby files of the same type are all represented by one taskbar icon as shown below:

Hovering the cursor over the icon reveals a thumbnail of each file. The advantage is that all the files can be closed with one click.

If you choose the "Never combine" option, grouping is turned off and all files will have an individual taskbar icon. The icons will also be larger, which can be useful for some users. The disadvantage is that each file has to be closed individually.

System Icons

Windows 7 comes with a set of new icons. These won't be to everyone's taste though, so fortunately it's an easy task to change them to something more to your liking.

To change the icon of a system folder, such as My Computer or the Recycle Bin, you first have to create a shortcut to it. To demonstrate this we will change the icon for My Computer.

Hot tip

If you can't find an icon that appeals, there are literally thousands available on the Internet. To associate downloaded icons with a program, in Step 3, use the Browse button to find and select the icon.

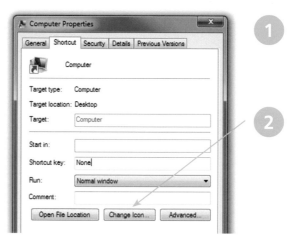

1 Right-click the My Computer icon and click Create Shortcut

2 Right-click the shortcut, click Properties and then Change Icon. This will open an icon folder

3 Make a selection and then click OK

Now all you need to do is delete the original My Computer icon. This procedure will work with most system folders. It will also work with third-party applications, most of which will come with an icon folder of their own (these will open instead of the icon folder shown above).

Folder Icons

Quite apart from changing icons for system folders and third-party applications, Windows allows you to change (and also customize) individual folder icons.

Do this as follows:

1 Right-click inside the folder you want to customize and then click "Customize this folder"

2 To customize the folder with an image, click "Choose File" and then browse to your desired picture

3 The image will be inserted into the folder icon as shown below

4 To change the icon itself, click Change Icon. Then browse to an icon folder and make your choice

Note that if you place a folder customized in this way on the Desktop, you may need to select a larger icon size to see the picture.

Using pictures is a useful way of personalizing folders, and also provides another method of identifying their contents.

79

Hot tip

Picture icons are an alternative way of identifying the contents of a folder.

Don't forget

You may need to select a larger icon size in order to see the image placed in a folder.

Uncover Hidden Icons

Windows 7 comes with hundreds of icons, all of which are stored in .dll files. The two main icon files can be located as described below:

While you can see the contents of Windows icon files, you can't move or copy them elsewhere. Should you wish to do this, download a DLL viewer from the Internet. These allow you to open .dll files and to access their contents.

1 Right-click any shortcut, click Properties and then click Change Icon. An icon folder will open

2 Another icon file can be accessed by typing: "C:\WINDOWS\System32\shell32.dll" in the "Look for icons in this file" box

If you have a DLL viewer (and nothing better to do), go to the Windows folder and open the System32 folder. Here, you'll find dozens of .dll files to explore for icons.

Folder Views

Having customized your folder's icons, you can now customize the folders themselves.

Menu Bar

One of the first things you'll notice is that the traditional menu bar is missing. We suspect that you'll want to get this back, so here are two ways to do it:

1. Open any folder and click the Organize button. Click Layout and then click Menu Bar. The menu bar will now be permanently restored on all folders

2. Press the Alt key. The menu bar will appear temporarily (see margin note)

Layout

To add elements to a folder window (or remove them), click the Organize button and then click Layout. The following options will be available:

- The Navigation Pane – this is enabled by default and allows you to browse the computer without leaving the folder. If you have no need to do this, disable it here

- The Details Pane – this is also enabled by default and is an advanced version of the old Status bar. It displays useful information, such as file type, file size, date of creation, etc.

- The Preview Pane – this needs to be enabled and allows you to see the contents of a file without actually opening it. Simply hover the mouse over the file

Don't forget

The Alt key method allows you to make only one selection before the menu bar disappears again. Each selection will require the Alt key to be pressed first.

Change Your User Picture

Each time an account is created, Windows assigns it a user picture to help identify the account and also add a bit of visual interest.

These pictures will be seen on the logon screen and at the top-right of the Start menu, as shown left.

Hot tip

Many people will prefer to use one of their own pictures. To do this, click "Browse for more pictures..." in Step 2 and locate the picture you want. Windows will automatically resize it.

The default picture is a rather bland and uninspiring sunflower. However, it's very easy to change it.

1 Click the user picture. In the dialog box that opens, click "Change your picture"

2 Select a picture, then click "Change Picture"

Advanced Appearance

Hot tip

Anyone who's keen to stamp their personality on the PC needs to look at the Advanced Appearance utility. For example, it allows you to change the background color of folders, the color of menus, the spacing between icons, plus many other tweaks.

An often forgotten about customization tool that has been present in all versions of Windows is the Advanced Appearance utility. You can access it from the Control Panel by clicking Personalization, Window Color, Advanced appearance settings.

This enables you to alter many Windows settings.

Display a Logon Message

In certain situations, it can be useful to greet users of a computer with a message when they log on. This might be something friendly or a warning of some description. An example of the latter could occur in an office environment where it is common for company email and Internet facilities to be misused by employees.

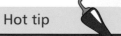

Hot tip

This feature is really intended for system administrators. However, you may find a use for it.

1 Open the Registry Editor and locate the following key: HKEY_LOCAL_MACHINE\SOFTWARE\Microsoft\ Windows NT\CurrentVersion\Winlogon

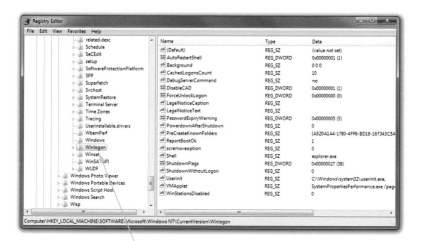

2 Click the Winlogon folder, and in the right-hand window double-click LegalNoticeCaption. In the Value Data box, type your caption, e.g. ATTENTION

3 Click LegalNoticeText. In the Value Data box, type the message to be displayed

Reboot the computer and your captioned message will be displayed before the logon screen appears.

Windows 7's Hidden Wallpaper

When Windows 7 is installed, a set of wallpapers is supplied that matches the locale the user selected during the installation procedure. Users who select US will get a different set than those who selected GB (Great Britain), AU (Australia), ZA (South Africa or CA (Canada).

However, all these sets are available if you know where to look. To uncover them, do the following:

1 In the Start Menu search box type C:/Windows/winsxs and press Enter

2 In the search box at the top-right of the folder that opens, type *.theme and press Enter. When the search is finished, you will see the following

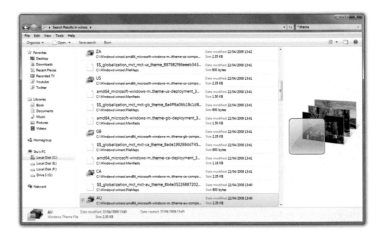

Double-click the US, GB, AU, ZA and CA theme files to install them. They will now be available for selection in the Personalization utility, as shown below:

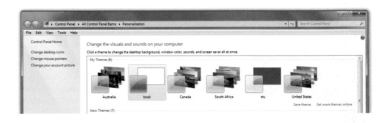

6 Paranoia

There are any number of reasons why a user might want to keep his/her activities private, both on the PC and the Internet. This chapter looks at the ways that users unwittingly reveal what they've been doing and shows how to avoid them.

Keep Your Activities Private

It's not easy to use a computer without leaving traces of what you have been doing. Windows keeps records of user activity in several places, and anyone who knows where to look can find out what websites you've visited, files you've accessed, programs you've been using, etc. If you're not careful, they can even access your password-protected web pages.

The following are the most common give-aways:

Jump Lists
When you right-click a program's icon on the Taskbar, a jump list of files recently opened with that program will be revealed, as shown left.

If you have been using Microsoft Word to type a letter to your Bank Manager, for example, a subsequent user will be able to see the name of the file in the jump list and also open it. To prevent this, do the following:

 Right-click the Taskbar and click Properties. Then click the Start Menu tab

Hot tip

Items in jump lists can be deleted individually by right-clicking and then clicking "Remove from this list".

However, one day you will forget to do it. This tip provides a permanent solution so you don't have to keep checking that you've done it.

Hot tip

Note that this action will disable the Jump List feature completely. It will still be there but with no items on it.

2 Uncheck "Store and display recently opened items ..."

Frequently Used Programs List

A feature introduced with XP and continued with Windows 7, is the Frequently Used Programs list. This list updates automatically according to the frequency with which programs are run.

There are several ways of dealing with this. The first is to simply right-click an entry and click "Remove from this list". However, it won't be long before it is back again, so this is not an ideal solution.

A more effective way is to disable the feature permanently so you can just forget about it.

Hot tip

Another way is to click the Customize button on the Start Menu tab of the "Taskbar and Start Menu Properties" dialog box. Here, you will be able to specify the number of recent programs to display. If you select 0, none will be displayed.

1   Right-click the Start button and click Properties. Then click the Start Menu tab

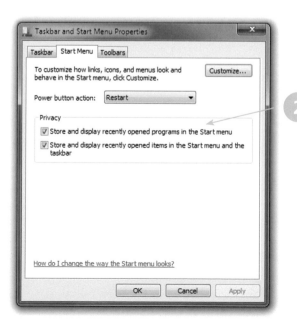

2   Uncheck "Store and display recently opened programs ..."

...cont'd

However, doing this will leave the Start Menu with a large blank area that you may not like the look of. Alternatively, you may find the feature useful and would rather just prevent certain applications appearing on the list. In either case, do the following:

1. Open the Registry Editor and locate the following key: HKEY_CLASSES_ROOT\Applications\Program name. exe ("Program name.exe" is the program you want to block, e.g. PhotoShop as shown below)

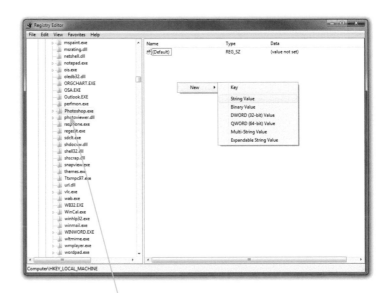

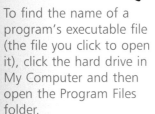

Hot tip

To find the name of a program's executable file (the file you click to open it), click the hard drive in My Computer and then open the Program Files folder.

Locate the program you want, open its folder and look in the Type column; the type you are looking for is "Application". Alongside this is the Name column which will show the program's executable file name.

When you name the key (Step 3) don't forget to add .exe after the program's name. For example: PhotoShop.exe.

2. Click the program's folder and in the right-hand window, right-click and select New, String Value. Name it NoStartPage

3. If the program you want isn't listed under Applications, right-click the Applications folder and select New, Key. Give the key the same name as the program's executable file (see margin note). Then follow the procedure described in Step 2

Reboot the PC. The application in question will now never be displayed on the Frequently Used Programs list – very handy for hiding from the boss the fact that you play FreeCell all day.

Most Recently Used Lists (MRUs)

The most common method of preventing other users from seeing a private file is to simply squirrel it away in a location that is not likely to be accessed by someone else – out of sight, out of mind, as the saying goes.

However, while a file hidden in this way may be difficult to physically locate, there is a way for another user to easily find it.

This is courtesy of the Most Recently Used files feature, found in most programs, that enables a user to reopen a recent file quickly without having to go to its location.

Hot tip

With most programs, the MRU list can be cleared by disabling the feature. The option for doing this is usually found in the Options menu.

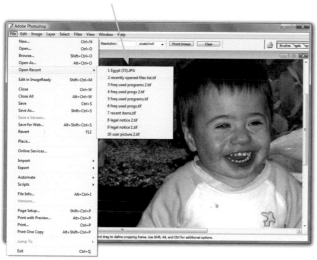

So a user looking to keep a particular file private will need to clear the MRU list in any program it has been accessed with recently – see margin note.

Windows Searches

Another method of finding data is using the Windows Search utility. No matter how well a user hides a file, if another user specifies that file type in a search, the file will be revealed.

For example, if someone was to type .doc into the search box on the Start menu, all Microsoft Word documents would be found.

The problem here is that there is no way to configure the Search utility to prevent another user from searching for a file of a specific type.

...cont'd

So the only way to prevent files being revealed by Windows Searches is to place them in a password-protected folder.

Users running Windows XP are able to password-protect folders but this functionality has been removed in Windows 7. The only way to do it therefore, is to install a third-party utility (see page 101).

Run Command History

The Run command is hidden by default in Windows 7. However, if you, or another user, has added it to the Start Menu (see margin note), be aware that it keeps a history. This can reveal to other users what files, and even web pages, you have accessed.

Hot tip

You can restore the Run command to the Start Menu by right-clicking the Taskbar and clicking Properties. Then click the Start Menu tab and click Customize. Scroll down to Run Command and check the box.

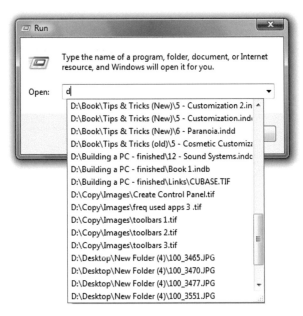

For example, someone typing the letter W into the Run box will see a list of all the web pages that have been accessed since the history folder was last cleared. Furthermore, by selecting a page and clicking OK, the web page will be opened in the PC's browser.

There is a registry setting that will clear the Run history, but an easier way is to download and install a program called MRU-Blaster from www.javacoolsoftware.com. This is a free utility that will clear not only the Windows Run History but also program MRUs (see page 89).

Hide Your Browsing Tracks

Browsing History

In the same way that Windows keeps records of user activity, so does Internet Explorer.

This information is held in the following places:

- History Folder – this folder holds a chronological record of every website and page visited

- Temporary Internet Files Folder – this folder is a cache of the pages you have accessed. Should you revisit a particular web page, your browser will retrieve it from this cache rather than from the Web. This makes access to the page quicker

- Cookies Folder – cookies are text files that websites download to your PC. They have several purposes; one is to identify you should you visit that website again. Often, they will also reveal the type of website, e.g. stuart@ luckydollarcasino

For users who wish to keep their Internet activities private, Internet Explorer provides a Delete Browsing History utility. To access it, open Internet Explorer, click the Tools button and then "Delete Browsing History".

The utility enables you to eradicate all records of your Internet activities, or just some of them by clicking the Settings button.

Beware

Don't forget to check your Internet Favorites. When accessed, certain websites will automatically place a link to their website here. Common culprits in this respect are porn websites. Anyone who happens to use your browser may see anything which has been added in this way.

Don't forget

The three folders that can give the game away for you are: the Temporary Internet Files folder, the History folder and the Cookies folder.

...cont'd

AutoComplete

Internet Explorer has a feature called AutoComplete that enables the browser to automatically enter web addresses, user-names, passwords, and data entered on web-based forms. This can be convenient as it saves the user from having to type out this information each time.

However, it can also be dangerous as it allows other people to access your password-protected pages, and see what data you've entered in forms, etc. It will also enable any snooper to see which websites you have visited, and any keywords entered in search engine search boxes.

If you wish to keep this type of information private then you need to disable AutoComplete or alter its settings.

Hot tip

The safest way to use AutoComplete is to disable the "User names and passwords on forms" option. Enabling it to remember web addresses is safe and can be very useful.

Hot tip

Disabling any of AutoComplete's settings will also remove any information previously held regarding the setting. It won't still be there should you subsequently re-enable it.

1 Go to Start, Control Panel, Internet Options. Click the Contents tab

2 Click Settings in the AutoComplete section

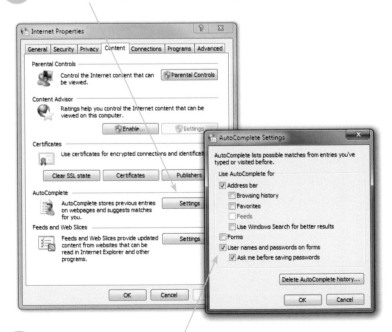

3 Remove the checks from "Address Bar" and "User names and passwords on forms"

InPrivate Browsing

As we have seen on page 91, it is possible to delete your browsing history after the session. However, there are two problems with this approach:

1) You may forget to do it

2) You have to delete the entire history when maybe all you want to do is to delete a small part of it – it's an all-or nothing action

The solution is a new feature in Internet Explorer 8 called InPrivate browsing. When used, InPrivate temporarily suspends Internet Explorer's automatic caching functions and, at the same time, keeps your previous browsing history intact. A typical example of when you might want to do this is buying a gift online for a loved one; once done, you can revert to browsing as normal. Your browsing history up to the point of opening the InPrivate session is kept but the InPrivate session itself is not.

There are two ways of opening an InPrivate session:

1 In Internet Explorer, click Tools on the menu bar and select InPrivate Browsing

Note that by default, the menu bar in Internet Explorer 8 is disabled. Enable it by right-clicking on the Favorites bar and selecting menu bar.

Beware

While InPrivate Browsing keeps other people who use your computer from seeing what sites you've visited, it does not prevent someone on your network, such as a network administrator from doing so.

Beware

InPrivate Browsing does not provide you with anonymity on the Internet. For example, websites might be able to identify you through your web address. Also anything you do on a website can be recorded by that website.

Right-click Internet Explorer on the Taskbar and select InPrivate. This will open an InPrivate session

A handy tip for those who will do a lot of InPrivate browsing is to configure Internet Explorer 8 to open InPrivate by default. Do this as follows:

Right-click the Desktop and select New, Shortcut

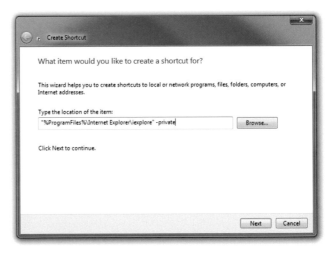

In the "Location of the Item" box, type:
"%ProgramFiles%\Internet Explorer\iexplore" -private
Click Next, name the shortcut Internet Explorer and then replace the original Internet Explorer icon with the new one

Hide Your Drives

The following procedure does more than just hide a file or folder; it actually hides the drive the file/folder is located on.

1 Start the Registry Editor and locate the following key:
HKEY_CURRENT_USER\Software\Microsoft\
Windows\CurrentVersion\Policies

2 Right-click the Policies folder and click New, Key. Name the new key Explorer

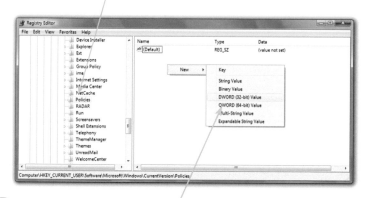

3 Click the Explorer folder and on the right, right-click and select New, DWORD. Name it NoDrives. Right-click NoDrives and in the Value Data box, enter the number of the drive (shown in the table below) to be hidden

Drive A – 1	Drive J – 512	Drive S – 262144
Drive B – 2	Drive K – 1024	Drive T – 524288
Drive C – 4	Drive L – 2048	Drive U – 1048576
Drive D – 8	Drive M – 4096	Drive V – 2097152
Drive E – 16	Drive N – 8192	Drive W – 4194304
Drive F – 32	Drive O – 16384	Drive X – 8388608
Drive G – 64	Drive P – 32768	Drive Y – 16777216
Drive H – 128	Drive Q – 65536	Drive Z – 33554432
Drive I – 256	Drive R – 131072	All – 67108863

Hot tip

To unhide a drive, you enter 0 in the Value Data box. Now, if you are going to be hiding and unhiding a drive on a regular basis, having to go into the registry each time will be a pain. So instead, you can create a shortcut.

Create a NoDrives DWORD, as described, and give it a value of 0. Then right-click the Explorer folder on the left and click Export. In the File Name box, type: Unhide.reg. Then save it to the Desktop.

Next, go back to the NoDrives DWORD and in the Value Data box enter the number of the drive to be hidden. Return to the Explorer folder and export it as described above, this time with the name Hide.reg.

Now just click the Hide icon to conceal the drive and the Unhide icon to reveal it (not forgetting to reboot).

Hide Your Private Files

Users who want to quickly hide a file or folder can do so by means of Windows Hidden Files and Folders feature. While this is intended primarily to conceal important system files, which if modified or deleted can cause damage to the operating system, it can also be used to hide other files or folders.

Hot tip

Another way to hide a folder is to simply squirrel it away in a folder containing a mass of other folders or sub-folders. Just don't forget where you put it.

Beware

The method described on this page, while useful, is by no means a secure one. Anyone who knows about this feature will be able to access anything you hide in this way.

1 Right-click the file to be hidden and click Properties

2 Check the Hidden box in the Attributes section and click OK

3 Press the F5 key to refresh the screen and the file will disappear

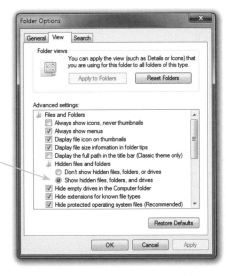

4 To unhide the file, go to Folder Options in the Control Panel. Click the View tab, and check "Show hidden files, folders, and drives"

7 Security

PC owners these days face an unprecedented level of threats to their data. Viruses are the obvious one and most people are well aware of this issue. However, there are many more and this chapter explains what they are and how to guard against them. There's also the issue of your children's safety; we see how to protect them from danger.

Secure Your PC Physically

One of the most glaring security loopholes of all is physical theft. The PC's data may be well secured but what's to prevent someone from simply tucking the system case under their arm and walking away with it? They may not be able to access the data on the PC but you've still lost it.

While your home insurance (if you have it – many don't) will cover the cost of replacing the PC, it won't replace your data. So if yours is irreplaceable, and you are not in the habit of creating up-to-date backups on separate media (writable CDs/DVDs, USB flash drives, etc.), or cannot afford to be without the PC for the length of time needed to replace it, then you need to physically secure it.

The following methods are available:

Alarms

These are the least effective method as they don't provide any physical restraint, but may be sufficient to deter the casual thief. A typical system will consist of a motion sensor that you fix to the system case. If someone tries to open the case or pick it up, an alarm will be triggered.

Cables

A cable system consists of plates, which are fixed to the case and peripherals by bolts or industrial strength adhesive. The cable is fixed to one plate, looped through the others and then fixed to an anchor plate on the desk. To steal the PC, the thief will have to steal the desk along with it. They can, however, open the case and steal all the components inside.

Enclosures

These are lockable heavy-duty metal boxes into which the system case is placed, and are secured to the desk by bolts or adhesive. This is the best method as not only is it impossible to steal the PC, it is also impossible to open the case and steal the PC's components.

So, if you want to keep both the PC and the data it contains safe, take steps to physically secure it.

Hot tip

Most laptops provide a connector to which a cable can be connected to secure them.

Hot tip

Locking devices for removable media drives are also available. These are mounted on the front panel of the drive and prevent access to it.

Restrict Access to Windows

The next step is to prevent access to the operating system. Here are three ways to do this:

Set a Boot Password

Most BIOS setup programs provide an option to password-protect the bootup procedure. To do this, start the PC and enter the BIOS setup program.

On the opening screen you should see an option to "Set User Password". Select this and enter a password; this password-protects the BIOS setup program. Then look for a security option (usually found in the Advanced BIOS Features page). This enables you to set a boot password. Do so, save the changes and exit the BIOS. Now bootup will stop at the boot screen and ask you to enter the password.

Set a Logon Password

This requires a password to be entered before the Desktop can be accessed. The option to set a password is offered during Windows' installation procedure. If you didn't do it, do it now as described below:

Hot tip

Password-protecting the BIOS setup program as well, means a hacker has two passwords to crack before the PC can be booted up.

1 Click Start, Control Panel, User Accounts

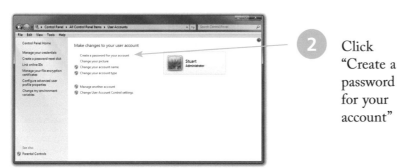

2 Click "Create a password for your account"

Hot tip

In case you forget your account password, you can make a password reset disk. This is explained on page 102.

3 Enter and confirm your password

...cont'd

Encrypted Password Disk

This is an extremely secure method of locking a PC by using an encrypted key.

<u>WARNING</u>: The procedure cannot be undone. Be quite sure that you need this level of security before you start.

Don't forget

Once you have secured your PC with an encrypted key, there is no going back.

1 Type syskey in the Start Menu search box and press Enter

2 In the dialog box that opens, click Update

3 Tick "System Generated Password" and then "Store Startup Key on Floppy Disk"

Beware

If you lose the disk containing the encrypted key, you will be locked out of your own PC. So make a backup copy of the disk and store it in a separate location.

4 Insert a floppy disk when prompted. An encrypted key will be saved to the disk

From this point on, every time you boot the PC, it will be necessary to insert the disk into the floppy drive before you can access the logon screen. So just make sure you don't lose it, otherwise you won't be able to access your own computer.

Password-Protected Folders

With access to both the PC and the operating system secured, the really security-conscious user may want to make things even more difficult for a potential intruder. The way to do this is to password-protect any sensitive data so that even if someone does manage to gain entry to the PC, they can't get to your data. Unfortunately, Windows 7 doesn't provide a folder/file password-protection function.

The only option therefore, is to use a third-party application. Do a Google search and you will find dozens of programs of this type. A typical example is one called Folder Password Protect, which is available from www.protect-folders.com.

This simple but effective application lets you password-protect any number of folders, either individually or collectively, by adding them to a main window, as shown below:

Click Next, and in the new dialog box enter the desired password. Click OK and you're done - the selected folder, or folders, are protected. To unlock a folder, click it and enter the password. It couldn't be simpler

Beware

A badly written password-protection utility can be more dangerous (in terms of data protection) than not having one at all. If it is buggy, you could well end up losing your data. For this reason, give freeware and shareware programs a definite miss.

Keep Your Passwords Safe

Having password-protected your system, if you now go and lose or forget a password, you'll wish you'd never bothered with it in the first place. This is very easy to do, particularly if you have several. So you need to guard against this possibility.

We'll start with your account password; Windows makes this a snap. All you will need is a removable disk or drive – this can be a floppy disk, CD/DVD or a flash drive.

1 Click User Accounts in the Control Panel and on the left, click "Create a password reset disk"

2 The Forgotten Password wizard launches – simply follow the prompts until the procedure is done. An encrypted key will be written to your disk/flash drive

Should you subsequently lose the password, you can use the disk to set a new password that will replace the original one.

While that takes care of the logon password, you will undoubtedly have several others, including your Internet passwords, e.g. eBay. Unfortunately, Windows does not provide a utility that can be used to safely store and manage passwords.

So what we suggest is that you acquire a Password Manager program. The easiest way is to download one from the Internet; you will find literally hundreds – some free, some not. The one shown below, Password Manager, is a typical example:

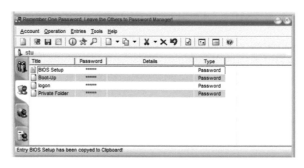

These programs work by hiding the passwords behind asterisks; a mouse click is required to reveal them.

Thus, malicious software will not be able to see what they are. The applications themselves are also password-protected to prevent physical access by a snooper. So all you have to do is remember a single password.

Beware

Keep your password-reset disk in a safe place. If someone else gets hold of it, they will be able to access your account by setting a new password that will overwrite the previous one. They'll be in and you'll be out.

Hot tip

Good password managers have an auto-fill facility, similar to Internet Explorer's AutoComplete. It should also be possible to install and run them from removable media. A good example is RoboForm, which can be used from a flash drive.

Encrypt Your Private Data

We've seen how to secure your data by password-protecting both it and the PC. What we haven't considered yet is the possibility of someone cracking your password. The answer to this is to encrypt the data itself, thus adding a further layer of protection.

Windows 7 provides data encryption via its Encrypting File System (EFS) feature and it's very easy to use. Simply right-click the folder containing files to be encrypted, click the Advanced button and in the dialog box that opens, select "Encrypt contents to secure data". When the encryption has finished, the folder's name will change to green to signify that it is encrypted.

However, even though it is encrypted, the data is still vulnerable to someone who either physically steals the entire PC, or the drive the data is stored on. This is due to the fact that EFS only works on drives formatted with the NTFS file system, so if the encrypted folder is copied to a non-NTFS drive, the encryption is removed and the data will thus be accessible.

To guard against this, you need to use another feature provided by Windows 7. This is called BitLocker Drive Encryption and it provides "offline" data protection by making it possible to encrypt an entire drive (including removable USB flash drives).

Go to Start, Control Panel and click BitLocker Drive Encryption. Click "Turn On BitLocker" next to the drive to be encrypted and then follow the prompts – this will include setting a password to unlock the drive. Note that the encryption process can take a very long time. When it is finished, if you go to My Computer, you will see that the encrypted drive now has a padlocked drive icon.

Hot tip

Note that BitLocker cannot be used on a single file or folder. You have to encrypt the entire drive that contains the data to be protected.

If you remove the drive and then re-install it, a dialog box will pop up asking for the password, as shown on the left.

To remove encryption or set a different method of unlocking the drive, re-open the utility and select "Manage BitLocker".

Data Backup

The final way in which your data can be compromised is by losing it. This can be accidental deletion, a virus attack, hardware or operating system failure, or data corruption.

As a safeguard against any of these potential threats, you need to create a backup on a separate medium. Apart from the medium itself, this requires a backup program. With Windows 7, Microsoft have provided a Backup utility that is not only extremely simple to use but is also very effective.

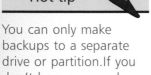

Hot tip

You can only make backups to a separate drive or partition.If you don't have a second drive, or one of sufficient capacity, we suggest you create a second partition on your existing hard drive and use this as the backup location.

Access it by going to Start, Control Panel, Backup and Restore. In the main window, you will see a "Backup now" button. Click this and by default, the utility backs up all data files, such as documents, images, videos, etc. When enabled, it runs automatically at a time and frequency specified by the user and simply updates the previous backup. You can also specify types of file not to be included. The backup can be used to restore everything or just selected files.

At the top-left you will see an option to create a system image. This will create a mirror image of whichever drive, or drives, you select. Should you have a catastrophic failure of Windows or a hard drive failure, this can be used to restore your computer to exactly how it was when the backup was made.

Note that with both options, you will need a different medium on which to store the backup, e.g. a second hard drive, a CD/DVD disc or a USB flash drive.

With this excellent utility, there is now absolutely no excuse for ever losing any of your data. When you first install Windows, we suggest you set up the PC exactly as you want it and then make a mirror image. Then enable the Backup Files option so that you always have a copy of your data files available.

Recover Your Data

With its Backup utility, Windows has the issue of data loss pretty well covered. However, it can be a long-winded way to go about recovering a single file. Windows has the answer to this as well.

This comes courtesy of the Previous Versions utility. This application is integrated with the Backup and System Restore utilities, and uses the data saved in backups and system restore points. With it, users are able to quickly restore files that have been modified, damaged or even deleted.

For the feature to work, i.e. for previous versions of a file to be available, you must have at least one of the utilities enabled – both, to get the best results.

In operation, it's quite straightforward. In the case of a damaged or modified file that you want to restore, simply right-click the file and click Restore Previous Versions.

You'll see a list of available previous versions of the file. These will be either shadow copies (taken from a system restore point), backup copies (taken from a backup), or both.

To restore a file, select it and then click the Restore button. If it's a backup copy, a Restore Files wizard will open – just follow the prompts.

If it's a shadow copy, the file will be restored immediately – this is the quicker of the two options.

In the case of a deleted file that you want to recover, right-click the program that the file was last opened with, or the folder it was located in. Note that a previous version will be available only if a backup or restore point was created prior to the file being deleted.

Beware

If you restore a file, it will overwrite the current version. As this action cannot be undone, make sure there's nothing in the current version that you want to keep. If there is, copy it elsewhere first.

Keep Windows Updated

You would be forgiven for thinking that we must have finished with security by now. However, there is just one more thing. Due to the ever evolving threats posed by malicious software, it's essential to keep Windows updated. If it's not, its security measures, good as they are, will eventually be breached.

While Windows 7 is currently a very secure operating system, rest assured that even as you read this, many people are working on ways to circumvent its security features as they did (successfully) with Windows XP and, to a lesser degree, with Vista. To counter this, Microsoft release a continuous stream of updates, which plug security loopholes as and when they are discovered. While these can be downloaded manually by the user from the Microsoft website, this method has two inherent disadvantages:

1) It can be a lengthy procedure so many people will quickly lose interest and simply not bother with it

2) The user will forget to do it, or not do it frequently enough

A better way of keeping the PC updated is to use Windows Update. The option to enable this is offered during the installation procedure and if you didn't do so, we suggest you do it now.

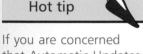

Hot tip

If you are concerned that Automatic Updates will slow your Internet Connection, you needn't be. The utility uses unused Internet bandwidth to "trickle-feed" the updates download without affecting the user's browsing activities.

1 Go to Start, Control Panel, Windows Update. Click "Change Settings"

2 Select "Install Updates automatically"

Hot tip

Windows Update is not restricted to just Windows. It will also update other Microsoft software on your PC.

Windows Update is a very good feature that works seamlessly in the background keeping the PC abreast of all the latest updates with no inconvenience to the user. Simply set it and forget it.

Computer Quick Lock

Another way in which the security of your PC can be compromised is by a casual snooper. They may, actually, not be snooping at all – it could be a family member who sits down at the PC while you've popped out to the kitchen.

Windows provides the solution with its Lock Computer feature. This is located at the bottom of the Start Menu and when activated, immediately switches the PC to the logon screen. Assuming a password has been set for the account, any snooper will be locked out.

Don't forget

The account must be password-protected before it can be locked. If it isn't, a snooper can just log on again.

You can also take this a step further by creating a shortcut on the Desktop or Taskbar that will enable you to lock the PC instantly, should it ever be necessary to do so.

1 Right-click the Desktop and select New, Shortcut. In the "location of item" box, type the following: rundll32.exe user32.dll,LockWorkStation

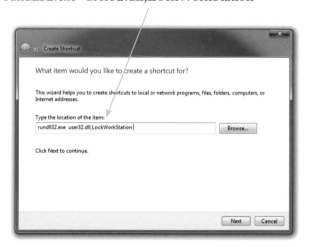

Hot tip

Be aware that there is a space between exe and user. The text must be entered correctly for the shortcut to work.

2 Click Next and give the shortcut a name, e.g. Lock PC

The shortcut icon will now appear on the Desktop from where it can be quickly accessed. Alternatively, you can drag it to the Taskbar.

Security on the Internet

Hot tip

Definitions are basically a list of known threats. As new malware programs are discovered on literally a daily basis, it's essential that Windows Defender is kept updated with the latest definitions in order to protect the PC.

Hot tip

Phishing is a scam that works by setting up a fake website identical to that of a respected institution, such as a bank (well, maybe not a bank but you get the point). Victims are sent an email with a link to the fake website asking them to log on. When they do, their username and password are stolen. The consequences of this are obvious.

The source of most dangers to PC owners these days is the Internet. Having learned from their mistakes with Internet Explorer 6, Microsoft provided Internet Explorer 7, and now Internet Explorer 8, with a whole raft of new security measures.

Before looking at some of these security features in Internet Explorer 8, we'll make a few general points regarding Internet security and Windows 7.

The first concerns Windows 7's anti-malware utility, Windows Defender. If you open this in the Control Panel and go into its Options menu, you'll see it's configured to do a quick scan. We suggest you change this to a full system scan. You'll also see an option that checks for updated definitions (see margin note) before scanning. Check that this is enabled.

The second concerns the Protected Mode feature. Briefly, in Protected Mode, Internet Explorer cannot modify user or system files and settings without user consent. Protected Mode requires the user to confirm any activity that tries to download something to the PC or start another program. By ensuring the user consents to these kinds of actions, the likelihood of automated and/or unwanted software installation is reduced. This feature also makes you aware of what a website is trying to do, thus giving you a chance to stop it.

We explained on page 62 how to turn User Account Control off completely. You should be aware that doing this also turns off Protected Mode, which is definitely not a wise thing to do. This one is up to the user – safer Internet browsing with the inconvenience of having to deal with UAC, or no UAC but a much higher chance of the computer being invaded by something unpleasant.

Also, consider the Smart Screen filter. This is Windows 7's anti-phishing tool (see margin note), which checks out every website you visit to verify its authenticity. However, it does result in them loading slightly more slowly than they would otherwise. If you are sensible enough not to need this feature, we suggest you turn it off. Should you wish to, you can use it on a site-to-site basis.

InPrivate Filtering

InPrivate Filtering is a new feature in Windows 7 that prevents websites from tracking a user's browsing activities and thus building up a profile of that user. This can then be used in a number of ways – some beneficial to the user and some that are definitely not.

Many people think that by disabling the use of Cookies, they are anonymizing their browsing but this is simply not the case. Another fact that most people are not aware of is that many sites these days are effectively amalgamations of several sites. For example, you may visit a site that you trust without realizing that some of its content is actually from a different source, i.e. a third-party site. Even if the content from the first-party site is safe, the content from the third-party site may be malicious. Furthermore, the first-party site will usually be unaware of this.

Don't forget

Disabling cookies does not anonymize your Internet activities.

Internet Explorer 8's InPrivate Filtering feature helps overcome these issues by providing users with greater control over which third-party sites can track and profile their browsing activities. It works by observing the websites you visit and building a table of the unique third-party content or object requests that are observed for each website visited. When InPrivate Filtering is active, third-party content is blocked based on a default threshold of ten unique observances of the content. (This figure can be adjusted by the user in the Settings dialog box.)

For example, if Internet Explorer observes that ten, or more, first-party sites that you have visited all load the same content from a specific third-party site, InPrivate Filtering will then block that content on all future websites you visit while the feature is enabled.

User "profiling" on the Internet is becoming increasingly invasive and the many people who are concerned by it will welcome this feature. However, it is turned off by default so if you want to use it, you have to enable it by clicking Safety on the Command bar and then InPrivate Filtering. Once enabled it will remain so until turned off again.

One caveat with this feature is that legitimate third-party content will also be blocked.

Don't forget

InPrivate Filtering has to be turned on by the user; its default status is off.

Protect the Children

The Internet is a minefield that can expose gullible and trusting kids to many different types of threat. All responsible parents will want to minimize, if not eliminate completely, the risks their children are exposed to.

There are many commercially available programs available that help them to do this, such as Net Nanny, CyberPatrol, Norton Parental Controls, etc. The best of these applications enable parents to control and monitor literally every aspect of what the typical child might want to do on a computer and the Internet.

However, this book is about Windows 7 so we will look at what this operating system has to offer in the way of child protection. We'll start with Windows 7's inbuilt utility - Parental Controls.

Go to Start, Control Panel, Parental Controls. In the dialog box that opens, you will be prompted to set up a user account for each child you want to protect.

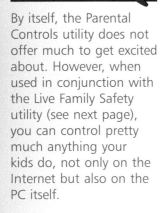

Hot tip

By itself, the Parental Controls utility does not offer much to get excited about. However, when used in conjunction with the Live Family Safety utility (see next page), you can control pretty much anything your kids do, not only on the Internet but also on the PC itself.

Having created a new account, click its icon to open the settings dialog box. Here, you will be able to set parameters such as time limits, game ratings, and which programs can be used.

However, this application doesn't allow you to control which websites your children can access nor does it provide a monitoring facility. To do these, and others, you need to fire up your browser and head to www.download.live.com. Download and install the Live Family Safety utility.

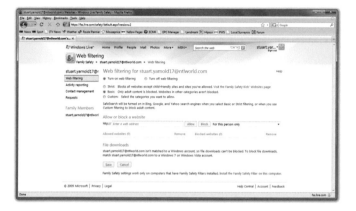

Don't forget

A big advantage of the Live Family Safety utility is that it is web based. This means you can monitor and control your children's Internet activities even when you are away from home.

111

This program provides a web based control panel (shown above) from which you can do the following:

- Block/allow specific websites

- Use web filtering to block unsuitable content. Different filters can be created for each child

- Block file downloads

- Control and monitor who your kids are communicating with via instant messaging software, such as Windows Messenger, and email

- Get monitoring reports on what your kids have been doing both on the Internet and the PC

- Access and adjust each child's safety settings from the Family Safety website, accessible from any PC

Used in conjunction, the Parental Control and Family Safety utilities not only enable parents to control everything their kids do on the Internet, they also provide a degree of protection to the PC by blocking potentially dangerous downloads, and access to programs and settings on the PC.

Risk-Free Internet Browsing

The Internet, as we all know, is the source of virtually all dangers faced by PC owners these days. No matter how tight your PC's security, no matter how careful you are, something nasty will slip through the net.

So how is it possible to browse without any risk? The answer is to use a virtual PC when on the Internet. To build one, you need a virtual machine application such as Microsoft's Virtual PC, or Sun's VirtualBox; there are many others as well.

These programs enable you to build a completely functional PC that runs within the program. Below, we see a virtual Windows 7 PC running on VirtualBox.

Hot tip

Don't confuse a virtual PC as discussed here with the XP Mode virtual PC discussed on pages 55-56. The difference between the two is that an XP Mode PC is tightly integrated into the operating system, thus what happens on it can affect the host as well.

By default, a virtual PC is completely isolated from the host PC (the physical machine), thus anything that happens on it, such as a virus, or malware, does not affect the host in any way.

Furthermore, as you can install and run programs on a virtual PC, you can use it to evaluate downloaded software, safe in the knowledge that if the program is buggy, or otherwise suspect, it cannot mess up your physical computer.

In fact, any action at all that you may be wary of trying on your main machine, such as changing system settings, messing in the Registry, etc., for fear of causing problems, can be tried out perfectly safely on a virtual machine first.

Hot tip

There are two versions of Microsoft's Virtual PC. One is the original program, which can be used to run an isolated virtual PC as discussed here. The second is a modified version, which is designed to be used with Windows XP Mode.

8 Installation/Setting Up

This chapter focuses on installation and setting up procedures. Among other things, you will learn the best way to install Windows, and how to create a hard drive partition.

Upgrading to Windows 7

When installing a new operating system, the option taken by most users is to simply install it over the top of the old one – a procedure known as upgrading.

The drawback with this method is that problems on the existing setup will be carried over to the new one. Typical examples of this are viruses and malware. There may also be third-party programs on the old setup that are corrupted and thus cause problems; these may also be carried over to the new setup. Furthermore, they can cause the installation of the new operating system to fail.

For these reasons, the best way of updating your operating system is to completely remove the old one first. Then you install the new version. This method is known as a "clean install". However, there is a drawback – the procedure wipes the hard drive clean of all data, so you first have to make a backup of any data you don't want to lose and then reinstall all of your applications.

Because of this, you may prefer to go the upgrade route, in which case we suggest you first carry out the following steps. This will greatly improve the chances of doing it successfully.

1) Optimize your hard drive by running a disk defragmentation utility, such as Windows Disk Defragmenter

2) Run a disk checking utility, such Windows Chkdsk; hard drive errors are a common cause of installation problems

3) Check your system for viruses; these can stop an installation in its tracks

4) Having made sure your system is free of viruses, uninstall the antivirus program. Alternatively, you may be able to disable it in the BIOS. Antivirus software is well known for causing installation problems

5) Remove all programs from your Startup folder

6) Disconnect as much of your system's hardware as you can. It's during the hardware detection and configuration stages of an installation that problems often occur

Don't forget

Before carrying out a Windows reinstallation, make sure you have backed up any data you don't wish to lose. While it's rare, an installation can result in data loss.

Clean Installing Windows 7

When a clean installation of an operating system is carried out, the hard drive is formatted. This procedure clears it, not only of the previous operating system but also of any problems that may interfere with the installation process and affect the new setup.

1 The first step is to make a backup of all the data you wish to keep

2 Start the PC and access the BIOS Setup program. Open the Advanced BIOS Features page and scroll down to First Boot Device

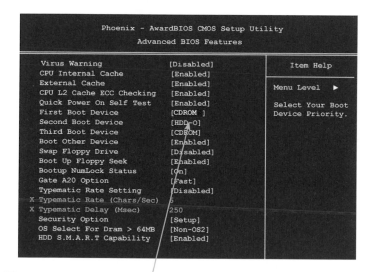

```
              Phoenix - AwardBIOS CMOS Setup Utility
                      Advanced BIOS Features

   Virus Warning              [Disabled]          Item Help
   CPU Internal Cache         [Enabled]
   External Cache             [Enabled]        Menu Level  ▶
   CPU L2 Cache ECC Checking  [Enabled]
   Quick Power On Self Test   [Enabled]        Select Your Boot
   First Boot Device          [CDROM ]         Device Priority.
   Second Boot Device         [HDD-0]
   Third Boot Device          [CDROM]
   Boot Other Device          [Enabled]
   Swap Floppy Drive          [Disabled]
   Boot Up Floppy Seek        [Enabled]
   Bootup NumLock Status      [On]
   Gate A20 Option            [Fast]
   Typematic Rate Setting     [Disabled]
 X Typematic Rate (Chars/Sec) 6
 X Typematic Delay (Msec)      250
   Security Option            [Setup]
   OS Select For Dram > 64MB  [Non-OS2]
   HDD S.M.A.R.T Capability   [Enabled]
```

3 Using the Page Up/Page Down keys, select CDROM, save the change and exit the BIOS

Having set the CD/DVD drive as the first boot device, place the Windows installation disk in the drive and boot the PC. Shortly afterwards, you will see a message saying "Press any key to boot from CD..."

Do so, and Windows 7 will begin loading its installation files to the hard drive.

4 At the first screen, click "Install now". At the next, select your preferences – installation language, time and currency format, and keyboard method

Hot tip

All the tools required to do a clean install of Windows 7 are on its installation disc. So, you must set the CD/DVD drive as the first boot device.

Don't forget

Should you subsequently need to boot from the floppy drive, you will have to go back into the BIOS and set the floppy drive as the first boot device, using the procedure described on this page.

...cont'd

5 At the next screen, "Where do you want to install Windows", select the required hard drive

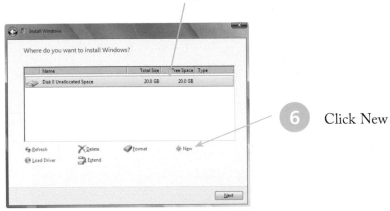

6 Click New

7 Enter the required partition size and click Apply. Then click Next

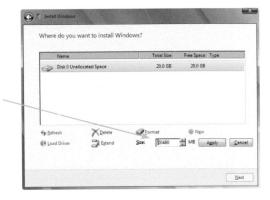

Hot tip

When you've completed Step 8, you can take the dog for a 15 minute walk. You should get back just in time to complete the installation by configuring a few settings, such as whether to enable Windows Update, and set an account password.

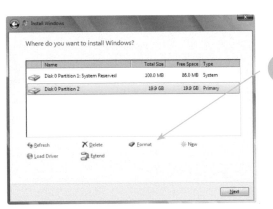

8 Click Format. When the format procedure has finished, Windows' setup routine will begin

Follow the prompts to complete the installation.

Drive Management

Windows Drive Management utility enables users to manage their hard drives. With it, they can create, format and resize partitions, create RAID configurations, and create and manage Mounted and Dynamic partitions.

Much of this will be well above the average user's head and is, in any case, beyond the scope of this book to adequately address. Therefore, we will restrict ourselves to a brief explanation of how to access the utility, how to create and format new partitions, and resize existing partitions. These are the applications that the typical user will be interested in.

1 Go to Start, Control Panel, Administrative Tools. Then click Computer Management

2 When the Computer Management snap-in opens, click Disk Management

3 In the main window, you will see all of the hard drives installed in the PC (one in the example below), plus the CD/DVD drive

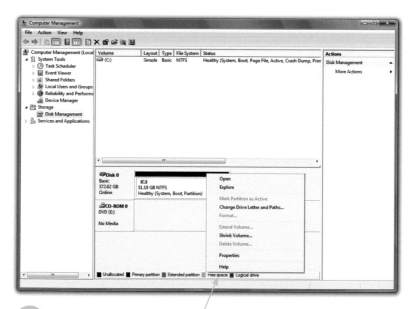

Hot tip

To avoid any confusion, note that the term "Volume", as used in the right-click menu shown on the left, is Microsoft parlance for a partition.

4 Right-click a drive to see the management options available to you

...cont'd

Hot tip

A partition is basically
a container within a
hard drive. Most PC
manufacturers supply
the PC with the hard
drive partitioned to the
maximum size, i.e. the
full capacity of the drive.
However, a partition can
be split into any number
of sub-partitions, each
of which appears to
Windows as a separate
drive.

Creating a Partition

First, please refer to the margin note for a brief explanation of
what a partition is.

In the example below, the PC has a single hard drive that has
been partitioned to its maximum capacity. This means it has no
free space. So before we can create a second partition on the
drive, we have to first create some free space to allocate to it. This
will be taken from the unused space on the existing partition.

1 Right-click the drive and click Shrink Volume

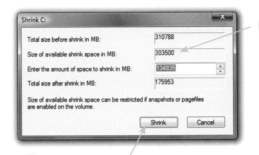

2 You will see
the amount of
space that can
be freed. This is
the maximum
possible size of
the new partition

3 Click Shrink. In the management window (below), you
will now see the amount of space that has been freed

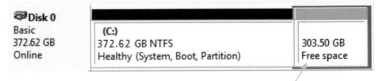

4 Right-click the area marked as Free space and select New
Simple Volume; a wizard will now open. Click Next in
each of the steps that follow and then click Finish. The
new partition will be created and formatted with the
NTFS file system. In My Computer, you will now see a
new drive – this is the partition you've just created

Resizing a Partition

To reduce the size of a partition, use the Shrink Volume
command. To increase the size of one, first create some free space
from a different partition, then use the Extend Volume command
to add it to the desired partition.

Hot tip

If you reduce the size of
a partition, the amount
it is reduced by will
become free space.
Unless you use this free
space to increase the size
of a different partition or
create a new one, it will
be wasted.

Setting up User Accounts

Windows allows the setting up of any number of user accounts, each of which can be individually configured in many ways (Desktop icons, wallpapers, screensavers, and so on).

This feature is particularly useful in a home environment where several family members all use the PC. By giving each their own account, which they can customize to suit their specific requirements and tastes, a single PC can be used sensibly and without conflict.

It can also be useful in a single-user environment by enabling a user to create accounts for specific purposes. For example, one account can be set up for photo-editing with shortcuts to all the relevant programs placed on the Desktop. Another account can be set up as a home office, etc.

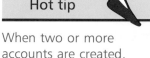

1 Go to Start, Control Panel, User Accounts. Click "Manage another account". Then click "Create a new account"

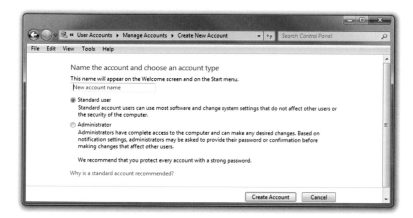

2 Choose an account type, enter a name and then click Create Account

3 To password-protect the account, click it. You will see various account options, apart from creating a password

Hot tip

When two or more accounts are created, one of them must be an Administrator account. The person running this account will be able to set restrictions on what other account holders can and cannot do.

Hot tip

A useful application of user accounts is to password-protect the main account and then create standard accounts for the kids. They can use the PC but won't be able to compromise its security or performance due to the limitations placed on standard accounts.

Keep Your Files and Settings

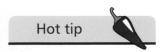
Hot tip

A USB flash drive is an ideal way to use the Easy Transfer utility.

One of these days you're going to decide that you need a new computer. Having bought it, you will then need to reinstall all your programs. You will also need to redo all of the customization and configuration settings, such as Internet/email settings, display settings, Taskbar configuration, and so on. The latter will be a time-consuming procedure.

Windows makes this easy with its Windows Easy Transfer utility. To access it, go to Start, All Programs, Accessories, System Tools, Windows Easy Transfer. A wizard will open as shown below:

Hot tip

Another good way is to use an Easy Transfer cable (this has a USB plug on either end).

The first step will be the Easy Transfer utility copying itself to a writable medium, such as a CD/DVD disc or flash drive. You then run it on the old PC where it will guide you through the steps necessary to save your old files and settings to the medium.

Then go back to the new PC, connect the medium and run the utility again. Your files and settings will be transferred and the PC will be set up exactly as the old one was.

You can transfer the following with Windows Easy Transfer:

- User Accounts
- Files and folders
- Program settings
- Internet settings
- Internet Favorites
- Email settings, contacts and messages

Run Older Programs on Windows 7

When you install programs on your Windows 7 PC, you may come across one or two that refuse to run; this will be due to an incompatibility issue with Windows 7.

Before you throw them away in disgust, try installing them with the Compatibility Mode wizard. This will recreate the Windows environment for which they were designed and will, in most cases, get them running.

Go to Start, Control Panel and click Action Center. At the bottom-left, click Windows Program Compatibility Troubleshooter. After a few moments you will see a dialog box showing you a list of all the programs on the PC. Select the one you're having trouble with and click Next.

Hot tip

Another way of applying compatibility settings is to right-click the program's executable (setup) file. Click Properties and then open the Compatibility tab. From here, you can choose an operating system that the program is known to work with.

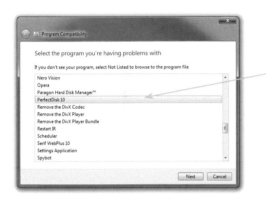

Select the program that won't run and click Next

Hot tip

If a program won't install at all, the method described on the left won't work. In this case, do it as described above.

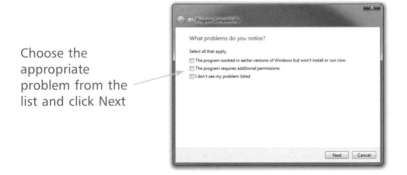

Choose the appropriate problem from the list and click Next

Hot tip

Once a program has been successfully set up, it will use the compatibility settings every time it is run.

Windows will try to fix the issue. If the problem hasn't been resolved, click "No, try again with different settings" to repeat the procedure with other possible causes.

Calibrate Your Monitor

Have you ever noticed when printing an image that the print-out looks somewhat different to the image on the PC? For example: it's brighter or darker, the colors aren't the same, or it looks washed-out.

It could be that the printer settings are not correct but it's far more likely that your monitor is incorrectly calibrated. Windows 7 includes a monitor calibration utility, and you can access it by going to Start, Control Panel, Display. At the top-left of the Display dialog box, click "Calibrate color".

Hot tip

Before calibrating your monitor, do the following:

Allow the monitor to warm up for at least a half hour so that it's at its full operating temperature. This ensures a consistent display.

Check that your monitor is displaying 24-bit true color or higher.

Set your Desktop background to a neutral gray. Bright colors and patterns surrounding an image make it difficult to accurately perceive color.

You will then be taken through a series of dialog boxes that will enable you to adjust your monitor's gamma, brightness, contrast, and color balance settings.

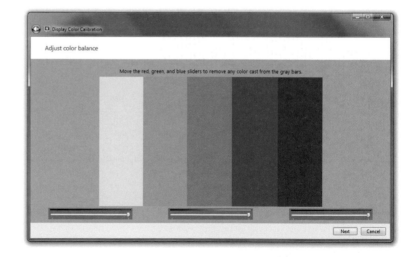

Install Windows 7 Quickly

This tip demonstrates how to install Windows 7 from a USB flash drive. The advantages of installing Windows in this way are threefold:

1) Speed – Windows 7 will install much quicker

2) You will have a much more robust copy of the installation disk (which you can now put in a drawer and forget about)

3) You can install Windows 7 on PCs that don't have a DVD drive

The procedure is as follows:

1   Plug the USB flash drive into the PC. Open My Computer and make a note of its drive letter

2   Open a command prompt by going to Start, All Programs, Accessories. Right-click Command Prompt and select "Run as administrator"

3   Type the following entries at the command prompt pressing Enter after each one

       diskpart
       list disk

You will see a list of all the drives installed on the PC. Determine which entry relates to the USB drive (see bottom margin note). Usually it will be Disk 1.

Hot tip

The USB drive must have a capacity of no less than 4 GB.

Hot tip

If you are not sure which is the USB drive, go to My Computer, right-click the USB drive and click Properties. Under Capacity, you will see the size of the USB drive. Go back to the command prompt window and the drive of corresponding size is the one you want.

...cont'd

4 Now format the USB drive by entering the following commands, pressing Enter after each one:

select disk x (x is the USB drive number, e.g. 1)
clean
create partition primary
select partition 1
active
format fs=ntfs
assign
exit

You'll now have a formatted USB flash drive ready to be made bootable. This is done by using the Bootsect utility that is supplied with the Windows 7 installation disk. Do it as follows:

1 Insert your Windows 7 disk into the CD/DVD drive and then change to the installation disk's boot directory where the Bootsect utility is located. Do this by going back to the command prompt window and typing the following, pressing Enter after each entry:

d:
cd d:\boot (d is the drive letter of your CD/DVD drive)

2 Still at the command prompt, type:

bootsect /nt60 x: (x is the drive letter of the USB drive).

Press Enter and close the command prompt window.

3 Now copy the entire contents of the Windows 7 installation disk to the USB drive

Your Windows 7 USB boot drive is now ready to go.

Before you use it, don't forget that you must first change the boot order in the BIOS so that the system will boot from the USB drive (see page 115).

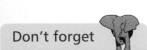

Don't forget

For this tip to work, the flash drive must be made bootable.

Don't forget

When using your flash drive to install Windows, you must first set the BIOS boot order so that the USB is the first boot device.

9 Shortcuts

Virtually every action that can be done with a mouse can also be done with the keyboard. This chapter shows how, and also explains some other useful shortcuts.

Switch Applications Quickly

Windows supplies three handy tools designed to help users differentiate between running applications and quickly switch between them.

Flip 3D

Hot tip

If you have recently bought a new keyboard, you may find it has a Flip 3D key. Many keyboard manufacturers are now providing this.

Press the Windows key and then the Tab key, and all open applications will appear in a stacked graphical representation on the Desktop, as shown below. Using either the mouse wheel or the Tab key, you can flip through the programs and select the one you want to maximise.

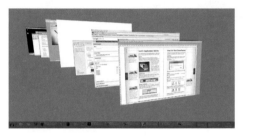

This feature is useful when several files of the same type are grouped on the Taskbar, as it enables you to see their contents at a glance.

Windows Flip

Holding the Alt key down while pressing the Tab key activates the Windows Flip feature. This is Flip 3D with a different view; operate it with the tab key and/or the arrow keys.

Taskbar Thumbnails

Resting the pointer over a Taskbar item displays a live thumbnail of the window that shows its content. The thumbnail is displayed whether the window is minimized or not.

Don't forget

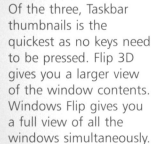

Of the three, Taskbar thumbnails is the quickest as no keys need to be pressed. Flip 3D gives you a larger view of the window contents. Windows Flip gives you a full view of all the windows simultaneously.

These tools provide several ways of quickly identifying what applications are running, their content, and selecting them.

One-Click Shutdown/Restart

Users who like to do things quickly will appreciate the following method of instantly shutting down, restarting or logging off.

Shutdown

Create a Desktop shortcut (right-click, New, Shortcut) and enter the text shown below in "Type the location of the item box:"

SHUTDOWN -s -t 01

Click Next and name the shortcut Shut Down. Then click Finish.

Restart

As above but this time type SHUTDOWN -r -t 01 in the box. Name the shortcut Restart.

Log Off

As above, but this time type logoff in the box. Name it Log Off.

When you have finished, you will see the following icons on the Desktop.

Using the tip detailed on page 78, you can change the icons to something more interesting or representative, as shown below.

Finally, drag the icons to the Taskbar where they can be accessed instantly.

Hot tip

You can also create Hotkey shortcuts for your new Shutdown, Restart and Logoff commands – see page 128.

Hotkey Shortcuts

There will be occasions when you want to open a program but don't wish to close the current window so that you can get to it. For example, you may be doing a tax return online and need to open the calculator.

A hotkey shortcut is the answer.

1 Right-click the program and select Properties

2 The Properties dialog box will open

3 Click in the Shortcut key box (this will be reading None)

Hot tip

If your keyboard came with a software disk, you may find that it contains a program that enables you to create hotkey shortcuts with the F keys.

4 Now press the key you want to use as the shortcut key (M in the example on the left)

Hot tip

You can use the tip on this page to open your favorite websites with a combination keystroke. Right-click a web page and select Create Shortcut. Right-click the shortcut, click Properties and then click the Web Document tab. Then follow Steps 3 to 6 to assign a shortcut key to the web page.

5 The Shortcut key box will now read Ctrl+Alt+M

6 Click OK, and from now on you can open the application by pressing Ctrl+Alt+M

Windows Key Shortcuts

Most standard keyboards have one, or even two, Windows keys. These are situated near the space bar and have a logo of a flying window printed on them.

Windows keys

With either of these keys you can quickly open a number of applications on your computer.

The table below shows which keys can be used in conjunction with the Windows key and what they do.

Keys	Action
Windows key	Open the Start Menu
Windows key+D	Minimize or restore all windows
Windows key+SHIFT+M	Undo minimize all windows
Windows key+E	Open My Computer
Windows key+F	Open Windows Search utility
Windows key+R	Open Run dialog box
Windows key+BREAK	Open System Properties dialog box
Windows key+L	Lock Computer
Windows key+Tab	Operates Windows Flip 3D
Windows key+T	Cycle through Taskbar programs
Windows key+Spacebar	Bring all gadgets to the front
Windows key+U	Open Ease of Access Center

Hot tip

You will also find keyboard shortcuts within applications. Alongside most menu commands, you will see shortcut key combinations.

Easy Email

This is a handy tip for those of you who do a lot of emailing. Instead of starting your email program each time you want to send a message to someone and then clicking the Create Mail button on the menu bar, you can achieve the same thing from the Desktop with one click. Here's how to do it:

Hot tip

With this tip, you can create instant links to your favorite contacts and place them all in a folder on the Desktop. Alternatively, you can use the folder to create a Taskbar pop-up menu as described on page 52.

1 Right-click the Desktop and select New, Shortcut. You will see the following dialog box

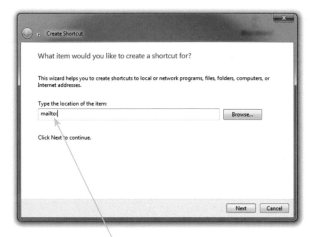

2 In the box, type: mailto: Then click Next and give the shortcut a suitable name

You will now see a new email icon on the Desktop. Click it and an open email message window will appear.

Taking this a step further, you can have the message window open with the address already filled in. Do this by entering the email address immediately after mailto:

For example, if you enter "mailto:stuart.yarnold@ntlworld.com" your email will open with this address in the To: box, as shown below. Then type in your message and click Send.

Taskbar Searching

A little-used feature in Windows is the Address toolbar. This lets you do a number of things directly from the Desktop.

Right-click the Taskbar and select Toolbars, Address. You will now see an address box on the Taskbar next to the Notification Area:

The first thing you can use the Address toolbar for is to launch websites; you don't need to open Internet Explorer at all. Just type in the address and press Enter, or click the arrow.

Furthermore, once you've launched a site in this way, you can subsequently relaunch it by clicking the down arrow at the side of the box and selecting the site from the History list.

You can also conduct an Internet search from the Address toolbar. To do this, just enter your search keyword and press Enter on the keyboard:

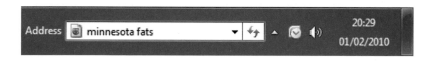

Internet Explorer's default search engine will open with the results of the search.

Finally, you can launch programs from the Address toolbar if you know their executable name. For example, typing "winword" will open Microsoft Word.

Hot tip

There's nothing you can do with the Address toolbar that you can't do elsewhere. However, it does have the advantage of being accessible from the Desktop.

Keyboard Shortcuts

In certain situations, using the keyboard can be a much easier way of controlling a computer. The following is a selection of useful keyboard shortcuts:

Hot tip

The following are some shortcuts that work with most applications:

- CTRL+O – opens a document from within a program

- CTRL+N – opens a new document

- CTRL+S – saves work in progress.

General Shortcuts	
CTRL+C	Copy the selected item
CTRL+X	Cut the selected item
CTRL+V	Paste the selected item
CTRL+Z	Undo the last action
DELETE	Delete the selected item
SHIFT+DELETE	Delete an item permanently
F2	Rename the selected item
CTRL+RIGHT ARROW	Move to the beginning of the next word
CTRL+LEFT ARROW	Move to the beginning of the previous word
CTRL+DOWN ARROW	Move to the beginning of the next paragraph
CTRL+UP ARROW	Move to the beginning of the previous paragraph
CTRL+SHIFT+ARROW	Select a block of text
CTRL+A	Select all items in a document or window
F3	Search for a file or folder
ALT+ENTER	Display properties for the selected item
ALT+F4	Close the active item or exit the active program
ALT+SPACEBAR	Open the shortcut menu for the active window
CTRL+F4	Close the active document
ALT+TAB	Switch between open items
CTRL+ALT+TAB	Use the arrow keys to switch between open items
ALT+ESC	Cycle through items in the order they were opened
F6	Cycle through screen elements in a window
F4	Display the address bar list in Windows Explorer
SHIFT+F10	Display the shortcut menu for the selected item
CTRL+ESC	Open the Start menu
F10	Activate the menu bar in the active program
RIGHT ARROW	Open the menu to the right, or open a sub-menu
LEFT ARROW	Open the menu to the left, or close a sub-menu
F5	Refresh the active window
ALT+UP ARROW	View the folder one level up in Windows Explorer
ESC	Cancel the current task
CTRL+SHIFT+ESC	Open the Task Manager
SHIFT when inserting a CD	Prevent the CD from automatically playing

Internet Explorer Shortcuts

F1	Display Help
F11	Toggle between full-screen and normal views
TAB	Move forward through items
SHIFT+TAB	Move backwards through items
ALT+HOME	Go to your home page
ALT+RIGHT ARROW	Go to the next page
BACKSPACE	Go to the previous page
SHIFT+F10	Display a shortcut menu for a link
UP ARROW	Move toward the beginning of a document
DOWN ARROW	Move toward the end of a document
HOME	Move to the beginning of a document
END	Move to the end of a document
CTRL+F	Find on this page
F5	Refresh the current web page
ESC	Stop downloading a page
CTRL+O	Open a new website or page
CTRL+N	Open a new window
CTRL+W	Close the current window (if you have only one tab open)
CTRL+P	Print the current page or active frame
ENTER	Activate a selected link
CTRL+I	Open Favorites
CTRL+H	Open History
CTRL+J	Open Feeds
ALT+P	Open the Page menu
ALT+T	Open the Tools menu

Working With Tabs

CTRL+CLICK	Open links in a new tab in the background
CTRL+SHIFT+CLICK	Open links in a new tab in the foreground
CTRL+T	Open a new tab in the foreground
CTRL+TAB	Switch between tabs
CTRL+W	Close current tab
ALT+ENTER	Open a new tab in the foreground from the address bar
CTRL+9	Switch to the last tab
CTRL+ALT+F4	Close other tabs
CTRL+Q	Toggle Quick Tabs (thumbnail view) on or off

Hot tip

Many Internet Explorer operations are actually quicker using the keyboard. For example, the Backspace key is much easier to use than the Back button. Also, try using the Up and Down arrow keys to scroll through pages. The Home and End keys are other useful keys that take you quickly to the beginning and end of each page.

Hot tip

The list on this page contains just some of the keyboard shortcuts available for Internet Explorer. You can find many more by going to http://windowshelp. microsoft.com/Windows (type keyboard shortcuts in the search box).

...cont'd

Using the Address Bar	
ALT+D	Select the text in the address bar
F4	Display a list of addresses you've typed
CTRL+ENTER	Add "www." and ".com"
CTRL+SHIFT+B	Open Contacts

Hot tip

Type the main part of an address and then press CTRL+ENTER. This will automatically add the www. and .com to complete the address. This only works for addresses ending with .com, however.

Windows Live Mail Shortcuts	
F1	Open help topics
CTRL+A	Select all messages or text within a message
CTRL+M	Send and receive email
CTRL+N	Open or post a new message
CTRL+SHIFT+B	Open Contacts
DEL or CTRL+D	Delete an email message
CTRL+R	Reply to the message author
CTRL+SHIFT+R	Reply to all
CTRL+F	Forward a message
CTRL+SHIFT+F	Find a message
CTRL+P	Print the selected message
CTRL+>	Go to the next message in the list
CTRL+<	Go to the previous message in the list
ALT+ENTER	View the selected message's properties
CTRL+U	Go to the next unread email message
ENTER	Open a selected message
CTRL+ENTER	Mark a message as read
CTRL+I	Go to your Inbox
CTRL+Y	Go to a folder
ESC	Close a message
F3	Find text
F7	Check spelling
CTRL+SHIFT+S	Insert a signature
CTRL+TAB	Switch between the Edit, Source, and Preview tabs
CTRL+W	Go to a newsgroup
LEFT ARROW	Expand a newsgroup conversation (show all responses)
RIGHT ARROW	Collapse a newsgroup conversation (hide responses)
CTRL+SHIFT+A	Mark all newsgroup messages as read
CTRL+J	Go to the next unread newsgroup or folder
CTRL+SHIFT+M	Download newsgroup messages for offline reading

10 Facts and Figures

This chapter looks at ways that users can get useful facts and figures, not only about their PC, but the subject of computing in general. We also see how to get more specific types of information. For example: statistics that will enable you to monitor the health of your system.

System Details

Windows provides two useful tools for users who need to get details about their system.

System Information

The first is the System Information utility. This gives detailed information about all the hardware and software on the PC. To access it, go to Start, All Programs, Accessories, System Tools, System Information.

Hot tip

The System Information utility is buried in the System Tools folder. A quicker way to access it is by typing MSINFO32 in the Start Menu box.

The main page gives a system summary that includes items such as the CPU, the amount of installed memory, details of the operating system, etc. An expandable category list on the left leads to more specific details of the system's hardware and software. System Information will also give you details about any devices that are not working properly.

Device Manager

The Device Manager, as the name suggests, allows you to view, configure, and troubleshoot the PC's hardware devices.

On the left is a categorized list of all the system's hardware. Expanding the categories gives details, and access to the system properties, of the individual devices.

Hot tip

The Device Manager is a very useful troubleshooting tool. If a device is flagged with a warning symbol, double-clicking it opens a dialog box that will tell you the nature of the problem, plus a suggested course of action.

The Device Manager also flags any devices that are not working with warning symbols, and allows you to install, and also update, device drivers.

Third-Party Utilities

While System Information and the Device Manager provide a lot of information about the system, there are many third-party utilities that go into much greater detail. One of the best is SiSoft Sandra (shown below); this is available at www.sisoftware. net. For really in-depth details about your system, it is a highly recommended download.

Hot tip

SiSoft Sandra is available in various versions. The Lite version, which is free, will give you all the information you need.

Video and Audio Codecs

A problem that many users encounter when trying to play a video file is that they get sound but no video (or no sound in the case of a sound file). The reason is that the file's codec (see bottom margin note) is missing. To resolve the issue, they need to download and install it. The difficulty is knowing which codec is needed.

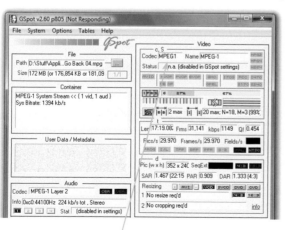

Go to www. headbands. com/gspot and download a program called GSpot.

Open the errant file with GSpot and you will be told not

only which codec it was compressed with, but also a great deal of other information about the file.

Then do a Google search for the required codec.

Hot tip

Another good utility is the Belarc Advisor. This is a free download from www.belarc.com.

137

Hot tip

A codec is a program that compresses the data in sound and video files, thus reducing the size of the files. When the file is played, the same codec must be installed on the PC in order to decompress it.

Windows Help and Support

For more general information, Windows provides a comprehensive interactive database related to understanding and getting the best out of your computer. This is known as Windows Help and Support and to access it, click the Desktop and then press F1.

Don't forget

Windows Help and Support is the place to go if you need assistance with any aspect of Windows.

Troubleshooters, how-to's and online help are all available here.

Microsoft's Knowledge Base

If you have an Internet connection, you have access to an enormous resource of information relating to all aspects of computers, the Internet, email, the various versions of Windows, and Microsoft software. This is the Microsoft Knowledge Base and you can find it at http://support.microsoft.com.

Hot tip

The Microsoft Knowledge Base is also a tremendous resource for computer troubleshooting.

Users who want to increase their knowledge of computing in general, or are in search of specific information, definitely need to take a look at this website.

File Information

Windows 7's folders give the user many facts and figures regarding their content. They all contain several default columns, each of which show a specific type of information. However, the user can remove the default columns if the information given is not required, and add other columns (by right-clicking any column heading) that give more pertinent details.

For example, the screenshot below shows a folder containing photos. Here, the default Tags and Rating columns have been removed and Type, Dimensions, and Date modified columns added; these give more useful information.

Hot tip

To see column details, you must select Details from the Views button.

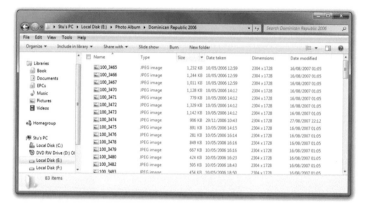

You can also use columns to organize a folder's contents. Hovering the pointer over any column heading reveals an arrow at the side. Clicking this reveals an "intelligent" menu that offers various options related to the types of file in the folder. This enables you to organize them in various ways. For example, clicking "Sort" lists the files according to their type. Clicking "Group" places them into itemized categories, as shown below.

Hot tip

The default columns you see in Windows folders vary depending on the folder's content.

Hot tip

Another useful feature is File Stacking. When you select this option, files of the same type are stacked on top of each other. Clicking a stack opens it to reveal all the files in the stack.

Gadgets

Gadgets are mini-applications that let you perform common tasks, and provide you with fast access to many different types of information. Typical examples are RSS news readers, weather forecasters, calendars, search tools, etc.

To use them, support software must be installed on the PC and with Windows 7, that support is built in to the operating system. By right-clicking the Desktop and clicking Gadgets you will be able to access nine pre-installed gadgets (shown above). Simply drag the ones you want to use on to the Desktop.

Windows gadgets cover a range of applications. The more useful of these are: a weather forecaster, an RSS news reader, a calendar, a clock and a currency converter.

A handy feature of Windows gadgets is that you can run multiple instances of them. For example, you can have any number of clocks, each set to a different time zone, as shown below:

Gadgets are also available from Yahoo (known as widgets); these require the Yahoo widget engine. Google do them as well (requires the Google Desktop).

Gadgets are both fun and useful. Give them a try.

Hot tip
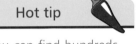

You can find hundreds more Windows gadgets online. Try http://gallery.microsoft.com.

Add Feeds to a Gadget

Probably the most useful type of gadgets are feed gadgets, which display automatically updated content on the user's Desktop. As we saw on the previous page, Windows 7 provides two such gadgets – an RSS newsreader gadget (called Feed Headlines) and a weather gadget.

The Feed Headlines gadget comes with preconfigured feed sources, which are unlikely to be what you want. To see what feeds are available for it, right-click the gadget, click Options and in the drop-down box, you'll see a list.

If you want to add a feed that's not in the list, you need to first add it to Internet Explorer's feed subscription list. Once you've done this, the feed will also be available in the gadget. The procedure for doing this is explained on page 153.

With regard to the weather gadget: to get a report for your locale, right-click the gadget and click Options. Then in the box, enter the required location as shown below:

Don't forget

To add additional feeds to a gadget, you need to first add it to Internet Explorer's feed subscription list.

Hot tip

Most websites that provide regularly updated content, such as news, sport roundups, share prices, etc., will also provide a feed with which to preview that content.

Click OK and from now on you will be able to access updated weather reports direct from your Desktop.

Monitor Your PC's Performance

The Task Manager

Windows 7 provides several methods with which to monitor what's going on in the system. While most of these are advanced utilities that are beyond the scope of this book, one that isn't is the Task Manager. Open it by right-clicking on the Taskbar and clicking Task Manager.

Hot tip

You can find more system monitoring tools by going to the Control Panel and opening Administrative Tools. Then click Computer Management.

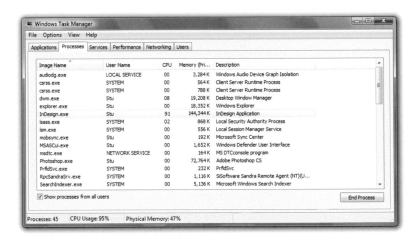

As an example of how this utility can be used to monitor your system's resources, consider the screenshot above. This was taken at a time when the author's PC was extremely unresponsive. The Task Manager showed why.

Highlighted, is a program called InDesign (a professional desktop publishing application used in the writing of this book). This was using 91 per cent of the CPU's cycles and 144,344 Kbs of memory (normally, it uses about 2 per cent of the CPU and 25,000 KBs of memory). As a result, the rest of the system was being starved of resources causing the PC to run very slowly. Closing the program and then restarting it resolved the issue.

With the aid of the Task Manager, you can make a note of the CPU and memory resources your more frequently accessed programs are using when running normally. If one of these programs should start misbehaving (a common occurrence with resource-intensive applications, e.g. PC games), and thus slow the system down, you will be able to track it down, and resolve the issue immediately.

System Health Reports

Another very useful information utility is System Health Reports. This provides a highly detailed system-wide breakdown that includes the status of the PC's hardware, system response times, and also suggestions on how to improve the PC's performance.

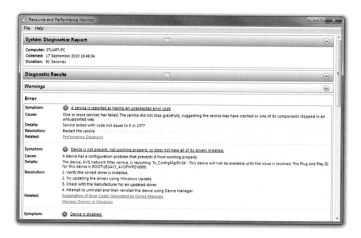

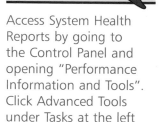

Hot tip

Access System Health Reports by going to the Control Panel and opening "Performance Information and Tools". Click Advanced Tools under Tasks at the left and then click "Generate a system health report".

Reliability Monitoring

Another useful set of facts and figures can be obtained from the Reliability Monitor. Go to the Control Panel and open Action Center. Click "Maintenance" and then "View reliability history". This opens the Reliability Monitor as shown below:

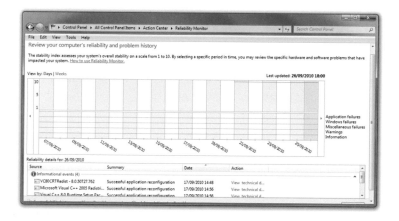

Hot tip

The Reliability Monitor also provides a summary of the system's stability. This is in the form of a System Stability Index rating, which ranges from 1 (least stable) to 10 (most stable).

The utility provides a day-by-day report on the system's stability and issues that affect it, such as program installations, and operating system, application, and hardware errors.

Laptop Battery Boost

One of the biggest problems with laptops is the battery running down. This is inevitable but by maximizing the energy efficiency of your laptop's setup, it is possible to considerably increase the length of time between charges.

To do this, all system components – including hardware, firmware, device drivers, applications, and services – must work in harmony. If just one component malfunctions with respect to power management, the energy efficiency of the entire system decreases.

Windows 7 provides a PowerCfg utility, which is designed to detect many common energy efficiency problems, such as ineffective use of suspend by USB devices, excessive processor utilization, increased timer resolution, inefficient power policy settings, and battery capacity degradation. Having analyzed a system, it then provides a detailed report that can be used to maximize a laptop's efficiency. Run it as described below:

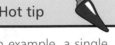

Hot tip

As an example, a single USB device that does not enter the suspend state can increase system power consumption by up to 25 per cent.

1 Go to Start, All Programs, Accessories, Command Prompt. Right-click Command Prompt and select "Run as administrator". Then, at the command prompt, type: PowerCfg -energy

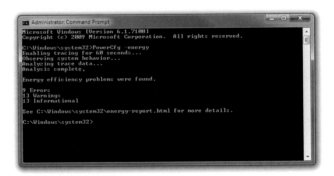

Don't forget

The laptop must have been running for at least 10 minutes before the check is run. Also, you must not use the laptop while the check is in progress.

2 The utility will check your system (this takes about 1 minute) and then generate the report

Then go to Start and in the search box type: C:\Windows\system32\energy-report.html. At the top of the window, you'll see "energy-report". Drag it to the Desktop and click to open it in your browser. By implementing the recommendations it makes, you'll improve the efficiency of your laptop, and thus the life of the battery.

Problem Steps Recorder

As the local PC guru you're probably resigned to friends and family pestering you for help with their computer problems. This is bad enough but when they are unable to clearly explain what the problem is, or what they've done, as is often the case, it becomes very difficult, or even impossible, to help them.

A little-known utility supplied with Windows 7 may provide the answer. When you get one of these irritating phone calls, tell the caller to go to their PC and type PSR in the Start Menu search box and then press Enter. This will open Windows 7's Problem Steps Recorder, as shown below:

Once they have this running, get them to reproduce the fault, or do whatever it was they did, again. The Problem Steps Recorder will capture every mouse click and keystroke. When they've finished, they press Stop Record and a report is generated and saved as a ZIP file. This can then be emailed to you.

When you open the report, you will see a detailed step-by-step list of every action that was made. Even more helpful is the fact that screenshots are included, as shown below:

Hot tip

This is useful for the reverse situation as well – trying to explain how to do something to the user. A series of screenshots indicating where to click will be much easier for an inexperienced user to follow.

145

Windows Remote Assistance

Even better than the Problem Steps Recorder is Windows Remote Assistance. This utility allows you to actually connect to another computer and view its Desktop on your own Desktop. Furthermore, you have control over the remote PC's mouse so you can physically sort out a problem for the owner while they watch.

Remote Assistance has been around in Windows for a long time now but setting up a connection has not been an easy thing to do. The version supplied with Windows 7 includes a new Easy Connection feature, which simplifies the procedure of setting up a connection enormously. It works as follows:

Both users open Windows Remote Assistance by typing assistance into their respective Start menus' search boxes and pressing Enter.

Hot tip

For Remote Assistance to work, both PCs must be running the same version of Windows.

To use the Easy Connection feature, both PCs must be running Windows 7.

1 At the remote PC, the user selects "Invite someone you trust to help you"

2 The remote PC user then clicks "Use Easy Connect"

3 A password is now generated, which the remote PC user notes and communicates to you (by email, phone, etc.)

4 At your PC, you click "Help someone who has invited you"

5 You enter the password given to you by the remote user

Windows Remote Assistance will now establish a connection between the two PCs. When this has been done, you will be able to view and operate the remote PC from your Desktop.

Easy Device Management

Another new feature introduced with Windows 7 is Device Stage, the purpose of which is to simplify user interaction with devices such as cellphones, printers, MP3 players, digital cameras, etc. Basically, it provides a one-stop solution for managing all tasks related to the device in question. It works as follows:

Go to Start, Control Panel, Devices and Printers. You will see a set of high-resolution icons for all the devices connected to your PC, as shown below:

Click a device icon and a new window will open from where you can access settings for the device, and its features. In the example below, we see the author's Sony Walkman MP3 player. At the top we can see how much charge is in the battery and how much storage space is available on the device. At the bottom are various settings that enable the device's contents to be managed. The options available vary according to the type of device.

You can also access your devices from the Taskbar. When you connect one to the PC, an icon will appear on the Taskbar. Left-clicking it opens the window above. If you right-click it, you will see a jump list (see left) of the options available in the main window.

Hot tip

Not all devices work with Device Stage. Support for the feature must be built in to the device by the manufacturer.

11 The Internet

The Internet is a wonderful resource for information, entertainment, software and business. This chapter details a wide range of tips that include extending the basic functionality of Internet Explorer, useful features of this new browser (and how to use them) and how to improve the efficiency with which you use the Internet.

No More Broken Downloads

Anyone who downloads data from the Internet will, at one time or another, experience the irritation of an unexpected disruption to their download.

Unfortunately, Internet Explorer doesn't have the ability to resume interrupted downloads, so you then have to start the process all over again. This is not too bad if it is a small download, but if you are downloading a large file you could have wasted a lot of time.

The solution is to use what's known as a "download manager". Programs of this type monitor a download and if it is interrupted for whatever reason, will resume it from the point at which the download stopped; thus, you don't have to start again from the beginning.

They also offer other useful features, such as automatic scheduling, automatic redial (for dial-up modem connections) and details regarding file size, download time, and so on.

One of the most popular download managers is GetRight (shown below). This is available at www.getright.com.

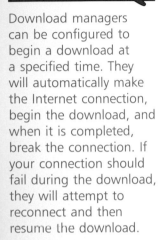

Hot tip

Download managers can be configured to begin a download at a specified time. They will automatically make the Internet connection, begin the download, and when it is completed, break the connection. If your connection should fail during the download, they will attempt to reconnect and then resume the download.

150

Hot tip

A handy feature offered by most download managers is the Drop-Target. This is a small icon that can be placed anywhere on the screen. Download links are simply dragged to it and then released.

A good download manager can also increase download speeds considerably. If the file is held on several servers (which is quite common), the program will switch between the servers automatically selecting the one that offers the best, i.e. fastest, download conditions.

Cut Down on the Scrolling

Have you ever opened one of those web pages that seems to go on forever? To find something specific, you have to keep scrolling down the page and, if you miss it, then scroll back up.

Let's say you are researching an article on Abraham Lincoln. Your search leads you to one of these long pages, the content of which is the American Civil War. All you want is info about Abraham Lincoln and his role in it, though; nothing else. So instead of endless scrolling down the page to find references to him, try the following:

1   On the keyboard, press Ctrl + F

Just above the page, you will now see a "Find" toolbar.

2   Type Abraham Lincoln into the search box

Hot tip

At the end of the Find toolbar, you will see the total number of instances of the keyword on the page.

151

Internet Explorer will automatically scroll down to the first instance of the word, or phrase, entered. It will be highlighted in yellow so you can't miss it.

3   To find the next instance, press Enter, and so on.

Utilize All Your Bandwidth

By default, the maximum number of simultaneous downloads possible with Internet Explorer 8 is two. For users of high-speed broadband, this two-connection limit is restrictive as it often doesn't allow the available bandwidth to be fully utilized.

For example, suppose your connection is capable of 2 MB/s and you want to download three large files from a website that offers a maximum download speed of 500 KB/s. Because of the two-connection limit, you have to wait for one of the files to be downloaded before you can download the third. However, if Internet Explorer would allow you to download more than two files simultaneously, you could download all three in the same time it took to download two.

Courtesy of a simple registry tweak, it is possible to configure Internet Explorer to allow up to ten simultaneous downloads.

Don't forget

Users of dial-up connections will gain no benefit by doing this as they do not have sufficient bandwidth.

1. Open the Registry Editor and locate the following key: HKEY_CURRENT_USER\Software\Microsoft\Windows\CurrentVersion\Internet Settings

2. Click the Internet Settings folder. On the right, right-click and create a new DWORD value. Name it MaxConnectionsPer1_0Server. Double-click this and in the Value Data box, set a value of 10

3. In the same window, create another DWORD value and name it MaxConnectionsPerServer. Give this a value of 10 as well

Reboot the PC for the change to take effect.

Keep up With the News

Many websites, such as news agencies, are now offering a service called RSS Feeds. This service automatically feeds information, such as news headlines, sports scores, etc., throughout the day to subscribers.

Internet Explorer has a built-in RSS reader that enables users to subscribe to, and read, any number of RSS feeds without having to visit the websites providing them.

To use this feature, you first have to find an RSS service and then subscribe to it.

1 When you visit a website that provides a feed, the Feed button will turn orange. Click the button to see what the feed offers, then click the feed itself

BBC Sport | Sport Homepage | UK Edition
You are viewing a feed that contains frequently updated content. When you subscribe to a feed, it is added to the Common Feed List. Updated information from the feed is automatically downloaded to your computer and can be viewed in Internet Explorer and other programs. Learn more about feeds.

Subscribe to this feed

2 A new window will open showing all the articles available in the feed. At the top of the window, you will see a "Subscribe to this feed" link, as shown above

3 Click the link to add the feed to Internet Explorer's Favorites Center and to the Common Feed List for sharing with other programs

To see a list of the feeds you have subscribed to, open the Favorites Center and click Feeds.

To view one, click it and Internet Explorer will open the page.

Don't forget

At the risk of stating the obvious, feeds work best with a broadband connection.

Hot tip

You can also configure Internet Explorer to play an alerting sound when you open a web page that contains a feed. Go to Internet Options in the Control Panel and click the Content tab. Then click Settings under Feeds.

153

Hot tip

You can use Windows Feed gadget (see pages 140-141) to read your feeds directly from the Desktop.

File-Sharing

File-sharing is a very popular Internet activity. It makes use of specialized peer-to-peer networks and software, which allow users to connect directly to the computers of other users in the same network. The purpose of it all lies in the name – file-sharing. Each user can designate specific files on their PC which they are willing to share.

To take part in this activity, you need a file-sharing program. These are available as a free download on the Internet and there are literally dozens of them (go to www.download.com and enter file-sharing in the search box).

Simply download and install the program, designate which files you want to share with other users, and you're all set to go. Good examples of this type of application are Emule (www.emule-project.net) and BitLord (www.bitlord.com).

Of all the file-sharing programs, Emule (shown below) is considered to be the best. It is also free of all adware and spyware, something that cannot be said for many of them.

When using these programs, there are two things to be aware of: First, some of them may install malware on your PC; be wary of this.

Second, while the use of the program is legal, the downloading of copyrighted material is not; you do this at your own risk. That said, many people use these networks and, if you are prepared to take the risk, an enormous range of music, movies and software is available to you.

Hot tip

To get the best out of file-sharing, you really need a broadband connection, as many of the files available for download run into hundreds of Megabytes.

Beware

File-sharing networks are awash with viruses and malware. Not only that, but the file-sharing programs themselves may add malware to your system. If you want to keep your PC as clean as possible, give this activity a wide berth.

Get More Search Providers

A useful feature in Internet Explorer is the Search utility. This allows users to search directly from their browser – there's no need to go to a search engine. Clicking the arrow at the right of the search box allows you to choose from a list of search providers.

By default, the only provider on the list is Windows Live Search (also known as Bing). However, you can add more as described below:

1 Click the down arrow at the right of the search box and then click "Find More Providers..."

2 A web page will open showing you a list of search providers. If the one you want is listed, click it to add it to Internet Explorer. If the provider you want isn't available then go to the bottom of the page and click "Create your own search provider". Then follow the instructions

Hot tip

When you add a new search provider to Internet Explorer, you are given the option to make it the default provider. If you do, all searches made from the search box will be conducted with this provider.

Hot tip

You can try the tip on this page with any website that has a search box. As long as the URL of the search results page includes the word TEST, you will be able to add it to Internet Explorer.

Quick Internet Searching

Type the word "tiger" in Google and you will get millions of pages to look through. These will range from the Tiger Lily restaurant in Shanghai, Tiger Woods the golfer to, not surprisingly, pages about tigers. Finding something specific will take a long time.

To help users narrow their searches, all the major search engines offer an Advanced Search. This will offer various options, such as language-specific searches, and searches restricted to pages updated within a specific time frame, etc.

Don't forget

Be aware that different search engines work in different ways. For example, with some, the + operator is used by default, while with others, it isn't.

However, before you try these, the following simple search aids may be all you need.

The + Operator

Most search engines exclude common words such as "and" and "to", and certain single digits and letters. If you want to make sure a common word is included in the search, type + before it.

For example:

world war +1 (make sure there is a space between the + and the previous word).

Hot tip

A "Search Site" feature found in the Google Toolbar (http://toolbar. google.com) enables a user to search within a specific website, even if the website does not provide a search engine of its own.

The - Operator

The - operator allows you to exclude words from a search. For example, if you are looking for windows (glass ones), type:

windows -microsoft -vista -xp -me -98 -2000 -nt

This will eliminate millions of pages devoted to the various Windows operating systems.

The OR Operator

The OR operator allows you to search for pages that contain word A OR word B OR word C, etc. For example, to do a search on camping trips in either Yosemite or Yellowstone national parks, you would type the following:

"camping trips" yosemite OR yellowstone

Phrase Searches

By enclosing your keywords in quotation marks, you will do a phrase search. This will return pages with all the keywords in the order entered. For example, "atlanta falcons" will return pages mainly concerning the Atlanta NFL team. Most pages regarding Atlanta (the city) or Falcons (the birds) will be excluded.

Combinations of Operators

To further narrow your searches, you can use combinations of search operators and phrase searches. Using our atlanta falcons example, typing "atlanta falcons" +nfl -olympic games -birds of prey will return about 1,300 pages as opposed to four and a half million pages for "atlanta falcons" (results taken from Google).

Numrange Searches

Numrange searches can be used to ensure that search results contain numbers within a specified range. You can conduct a numrange search by specifying two numbers, separated by two periods with no spaces.

For example, you would search for computers in the $600 to $900 price bracket by typing: computers $600..900

Numrange can be used for all types of units (monetary, weight, measurement, and so on).

Hot tip

You may, at some stage, come across the phrase "Boolean Operators" with regard to search engines. These are derived from Boolean Logic, which is a system for establishing relationships between terms. The three main Boolean operators are:

- OR
- AND (equivalent to +)
- NOT (equivalent to -)

Hot tip

The most useful operators are: - (NOT), and quotation marks (phrase searching). These two operators can whittle a search, that would otherwise be several million, down to a few hundred pages.

Repairing Internet Explorer

Internet Explorer is a highly complex piece of software and (as with Windows itself) can, over time, become corrupted to the extent that it no longer works properly or little niggles and errors creep in.

Should you find yourself in this situation, try the following:

Disable All Add-Ons

While browser add-ons can enhance your browsing, they do sometimes conflict with other software on your computer. To eliminate these as a possible source of the problem, try running Internet Explorer without any add-ons.

Do it by going to Start, All Programs, Accessories, System Tools, Internet Explorer (No Add-ons). If this resolves the problem, start Internet Explorer as usual (add-ons enabled) and then use the Add-ons Manager (Tools, Manage Add-ons, Enable or Disable Add-ons) to disable them one by one until the offender has been identified.

Reset Internet Explorer

If disabling add-ons doesn't solve the problem, try resetting Internet Explorer back to its default settings.

Hot tip

If Internet Explorer stops responding repeatedly, try the following:

• Scan the PC for malware
• Clear the contents of the Temporary Internet Files folder

Hot tip

Resetting Internet Explorer removes all changes that have been made to its settings from the time of its installation. It does not delete your Favorites and Feeds though.

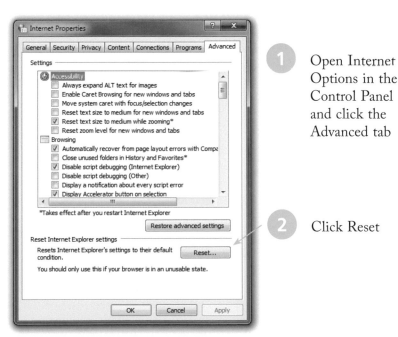

1. Open Internet Options in the Control Panel and click the Advanced tab

2. Click Reset

Get to Grips With Tabs

Browser tabs are another useful feature in Internet Explorer. Using them is straightforward enough so rather than describe the obvious, we'll show you some neat tricks that you may not have noticed yet.

Multiple Home Pages

Rather than have Internet Explorer open with one default page, tabs allow you to set as many as you want. Open the Internet Options utility in the Control Panel and in the Home Page box on the General tab, type in the addresses of the websites (when you've typed one, press Enter and then type the next one, and so on).

The next time you open Internet Explorer, it will automatically open all the websites, each in a separate tabbed window.

Categorized Groups of Tabs

Let's say you like to dabble in stocks and shares. You use the Internet for your share dealings and probably have several related websites in your list of Favorites.

Rather than open each website individually as you would have done previously, tabs allow you to open them all simultaneously.

To do it, open all the websites in separate tabs and click "Add to Favorites". Then click "Add Tab Group to Favorites". In the next dialog box, enter a name for the group, e.g. Stocks. Then click Add.

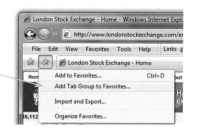

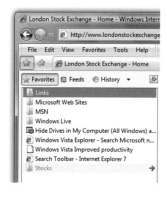

The next time you want to see how your shares are doing, click the Favorites button and then click the arrow alongside your Stocks folder. All the websites in the group will now open in separate tabbed windows. Alternatively, click the folder itself to show a list of all the websites. From here, you can open any of them individually.

Hot tip

To close a specific tab when you have several open, you have to click the tab in order to reveal the X button. A quicker way is to click anywhere in the tab with the mouse's scroll wheel.

Back up Your Favorites

A large, well organized list of Favorites takes a long time to build up and is literally impossible to replace. Losing it can be nothing short of a calamity.

If you have such a list and don't relish the prospect of having to build it up again, back it up as follows:

Hot tip
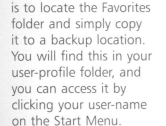

Another method of backing up your Favorites is to locate the Favorites folder and simply copy it to a backup location. You will find this in your user-profile folder, and you can access it by clicking your user-name on the Start Menu.

1 From the File menu, click Import and Export; this opens the Import/Export wizard. Click Next and you will be presented with three options

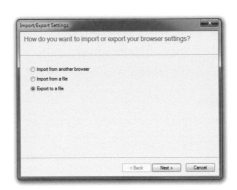

2 Select "Export to a file"

3 Select the Favorites folder to back up everything

Hot tip
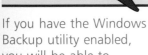

If you have the Windows Backup utility enabled, you will be able to restore your Favorites from the backup file.

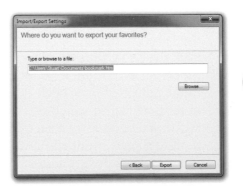

4 Browse to your backup location. Click Next and then Finish

Enhance Internet Explorer

Utilities

Good program that it undoubtedly is, Internet Explorer still has room for improvement. One way of doing this is by means of browser add-ons.

Go to www.ieaddons.com and you will find a large range of third-party utilities (many of them free) that will enable you to increase the functionality of Internet Explorer considerably.

Typical examples include toolbars, malware removal utilities, pop-up blockers, password managers, media players and many more.

Java Virtual Machine

Many websites use Java applets, e.g. calenders, games, digital clocks, etc. For these to work, the browser being used to view them must have a Java Virtual Machine installed.

Earlier versions of Internet Explorer had Microsoft's version of Java VM but Internet Explorer 8 does not. The only way to get your browser Java enabled now is to download Sun Microsystem's Java VM from www.java.com.

It's not a major deal if you don't have it, as relatively few websites use Java applets but, as it's a free download, you may as well have it. When you do visit a website that uses Java, you'll be ready.

Hot tip

Two other add-ons that are used by many websites are: Adobe Flash Player and Adobe Shockwave Player. These can be downloaded from www.adobe.com.

Web Slices

A Web Slice is similar to an RSS feed. Basically, it lets you subscribe to a specific section of a web page and then alerts you when the content of the slice has changed; for example, the current temperature, or an auction price.

When you visit a web page that offers slices, you will see a green icon on the Command bar, as shown below:

Hot tip

A list of websites that provide Web Slices can be found at: www.ieaddons.com/en/webslices.

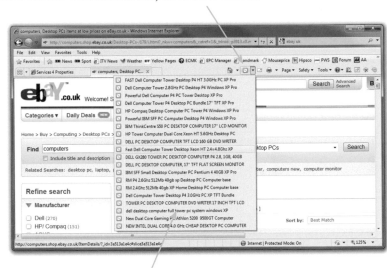

Click the side arrow to reveal the available slices

To subscribe to a slice, just click it. It will be added as a link on the Favorites bar, as shown below:

When the Web Slice is updated, the link on the Favorites bar will appear with bold formatting. You can then click the link to see the updated content.

To delete a slice when you've finished with it, right-click it on the Favorites bar and click Delete.

Speed up Internet Explorer

On page 161, we show how browser add-ons can extend the versatility and capability of Internet Explorer. Typical add-ons include toolbars, download managers, Adobe Reader, etc.

The negative aspect of these add-ons is that they all take time to load, and thus prevent Internet Explorer from starting as fast (and often running) as it otherwise might. They can also be the cause of other problems, such as pop-up advertisments, browser lock-ups, and even a reduction in the performance of the PC.

If you are having problems with your browsing, or just want Internet Explorer to run as fast as possible, you have two options:

The first is to go to the menu bar and click Tools, Manage Add-ons. You will see a list of all the add-ons installed on Internet Explorer, as shown below:

By selecting each add-on in turn and clicking the Disable button, you can run Internet Explorer without any, or just some, add-ons, and thus eliminate potential causes of Internet-related issues.

Another thing you can do in the Manage Add-ons window is check how long it takes for each add-on to load. This information is available in the Load Time column. If you see one that is taking an abnormal length of time to load in comparison to the others, try disabling just this one.

The second (and easiest) option is to go to Start, All Programs, Accessories, System Tools, Internet Explorer (No Add-ons). This runs Internet Explorer with all add-ons automatically disabled.

Accelerate Your Browsing

Finding what you want on the Internet can be a long-winded procedure that involves moving from one site to another. For example, you may be on holiday and want to identify and then locate a good restaurant.

First you have to decide which restaurant you are going to use by doing a search engine search. Having established this, you then use a different site, e.g. Google Maps, to find out how to get to it.

Internet Explorer's Accelerator feature allows you to do both without leaving the first site. Using our restaurant example, you have picked one called The Four Seasons. Highlight the name and you will see a blue accelerator icon appear to the side of it.

Hot tip

A list of accelerators can be found at www.ieaddons.com/us/accelerators.

Click the icon and you will see a list of accelerators installed in Internet Explorer. Select "Map with Live Search" and a map of the restaurant's location will be generated and displayed.

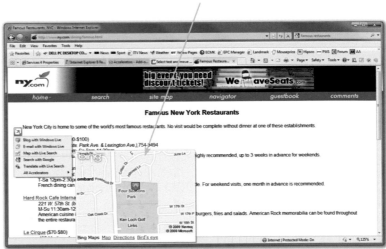

Clicking the map will open a full webpage in a new tab that includes additional information from the mapping service.

This is just one example of how accelerators can be used.

Easy Text Selection

When selecting text in a web page it can be difficult to select precisely what you want without also selecting adjacent text, and objects such as images and tables, as shown below:

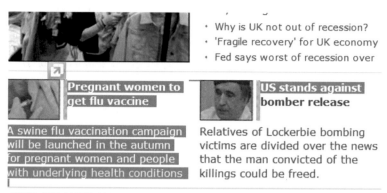

Internet Explorer's Caret Browsing feature has been introduced to solve this problem. This enables you to use the keyboard instead of the mouse to make selections, and it offers much more precise control.

To activate Caret Browsing, press F7. Then place the cursor at the beginning of the text block you want to select, press and hold down the Shift key and highlight the text with the arrow keys.

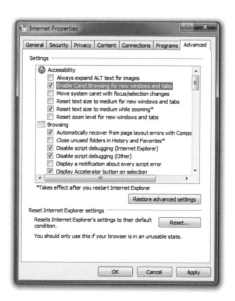

Some users may find this feature so useful that they might want to have Caret Browsing permanently enabled. This is very easy to do.

On Internet Explorer's menu bar, click Tools, Internet Options. Then click the Advanced tab and check "Enable Caret Browsing ..."

Hot tip

Caret browsing can be enabled on a per-tab basis or for all tabs and windows.

Miscellaneous Tips

Quick Printing

Rather than print out an entire page when all you want is a few lines or a paragraph, do the following:

Hot tip

Virtually all web pages have useless headers and footers that print along with the page contents. Prevent this by clicking the "Turn header and footers off" button on the Print Preview toolbar.

1 Select the required text, right-click and select Print

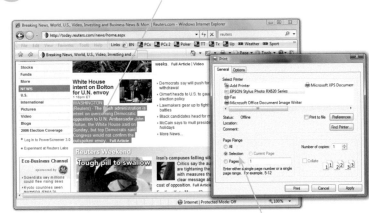

2 In the printer's software, select Selection. Only the selected text will be printed

Print Scaling

When you print a web page, Internet Explorer automatically scales it to fit within the margins of your paper. Should you prefer to do this yourself, however, do the following.

1 Click the arrow next to the Print button and click "Print Preview"

2 In the Print Preview window, grab the resize handles and drag them to resize the page

Stop Script Debugging Error Messages

A problem that can occur when browsing the Internet with Internet Explorer is the sudden appearance of "Script Debug" error messages. These usually say something like "Script error at line 01. Do you wish to debug?" These messages can be persistent and extremely irritating.

1 Go to Start, Control Panel, Internet Options. Click the Advanced tab

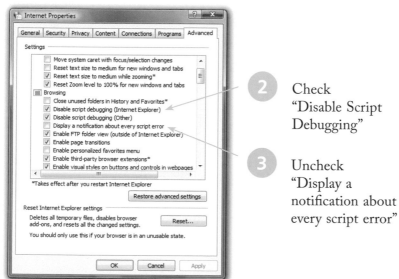

2 Check "Disable Script Debugging"

3 Uncheck "Display a notification about every script error"

Hot tip

Internet Explorer's Script Debugging utility is a troubleshooting tool designed for website developers. For the average user it serves no purpose at all. Although it is disabled by default, some programs can enable it. So if these messages suddenly start appearing, disable it as described on the left.

167

Easy Web Page Links

Here's a quick way to insert a link to a web page in an email. Open the page, click Page on the toolbar and then click "Send Link by E-mail." An email message box will now open with the link inserted. (You can also send an entire page in this way.)

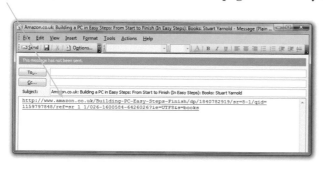

Get in Close

Internet Explorer allows users to zoom in on a page. This is useful for those whose sight is not so good or where text is hard to read.

Hot tip

You can also control the Zoom function with the keyboard:

- CTRL+PLUS SIGN = zoom in by ten per cent

- CTRL+MINUS SIGN = zoom out by ten per cent

- CTRL+0 = zoom to 100 per cent

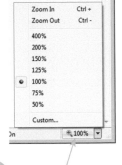

 Click the Page button and then select the zoom level required

2 Another way is to click the Zoom button at the bottom-right of the page

Stop the Kids Downloading

Have you ever worried about what the little horrors are downloading while you're not around? This tip will put your fears to rest.

1 Go to Internet Options in the Control Panel. Click the Security tab, click the Custom Level button and then scroll down to the Downloads section

Hot tip

The Parental Controls and Live Family Safety utilities provide another way of preventing your kids from downloading from the Internet.

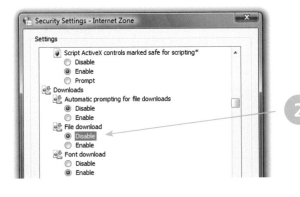

2 Under File download, select Disable

Override Disabled Right-Click Menus

Have you ever visited a website that has the right-click menu disabled, thus preventing you from copying or downloading? Well, in case you ever come across another of these websites, you'll be pleased to know there is a solution.

All you have to do is use the Context Menu key on your keyboard. This is located between the right-hand Windows logo key and the Ctrl key.

Just press it to bring up the right-click menu. Another, more laborious, way is to simply download the entire page using the File, Save As, command.

Image Resizing

Internet Explorer has a feature called Automatic Image Resizing, the purpose of which is to resize a picture if it is too large to fully display in the browser window.

If you don't want this, there are two ways to deal with it:

1) Position the pointer over the image and it will turn into a mini magnifying glass. Simply click the image to restore it to its full size

2) Disable the feature. Do this by going to Internet Options in the Control Panel. Click the Advanced tab and scroll to the Multimedia section. Here, you will find the disable option

Hot tip

Another way to open the right-click menu is by pressing the Shift key in conjunction with the F10 key.

169

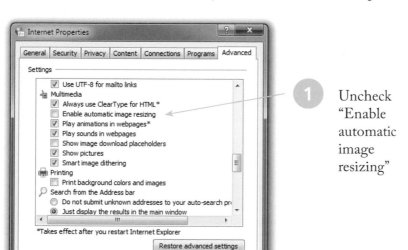

1 Uncheck "Enable automatic image resizing"

Hot tip

The Links toolbar is a very useful feature that enables you to create, and quickly access, shortcuts to your favorite websites. To open it, right-click the main toolbar and click Links. Now you will be able to drag the Links toolbar to wherever you want it. You can add shortcuts to it by dragging & dropping.

...cont'd

Researching With Internet Explorer

Internet Explorer has a Research feature that is designed for people who use the Internet for research purposes.

1 Click the Research button at the far right of the toolbar. If you don't see it, click the chevrons to reveal it

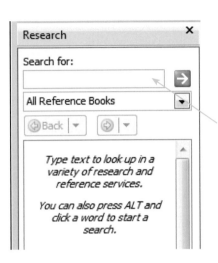

2 The Research window will now open on the left of the browser

3 Type a keyword in the box and Internet Explorer will search a list of selected websites. To see what these are, click the arrow next to All Reference Books

---

Hot tip

At the bottom of the Research pane, you will see a Research Options button. Click this to reveal a list of more websites that can be searched.

Emailing From Internet Explorer

If you would like to be able to send and receive emails while browsing the Internet, do the following:

1 Right-click the toolbar and select Customize Command Bar. Then click "Add or Remove Commands..."

Hot tip

Note that unless you specify otherwise, the Read Mail button will be placed at the end of the toolbar after the Research button. So you may need to click the chevrons to reveal it.

2 Select Read Mail under Available toolbar buttons and then click Add to add it to the toolbar. Now you will be able to open your email program from Internet Explorer

12 Email

In this chapter, we look at probably the most popular PC application of all – email. Learn how to safeguard your messages, contacts and account settings, how to access your email from anywhere in the world, beat the spammers, avoid virus attacks, plus much more.

Get Your Email Back

One of the first things you will notice with Windows 7 is that it does not provide an email program – you have to install one yourself. Here, you have a number of choices:

Mozilla, authors of the Firefox web browser, provide the Thunderbird email client, while another free email program with a very good reputation is Eudora. Both of these are good choices and can be downloaded from the manufacturers' websites. If you do an Internet search, you will also find a multitude of other email programs. This might be a good time to try out a few and see how you get on with them.

Alternatively, you can opt to stay with Microsoft. Their current free offering is Windows Live Mail, an updated version of the Windows Mail program that was provided with Windows Vista.

If you are migrating from Vista and used Windows Mail, you will probably decide to go with Windows Live Mail. This can be downloaded from the Windows Live Essentials website at www.download.live.com.

Setting up an account in Windows Live Mail couldn't be simpler; all you need to do is enter your email address and ISP password and then click Next. The account will be created almost instantly.

Hot tip

The menu bar in Windows Live Mail is disabled by default. Get it back by clicking the Menu icon at the top-right and then clicking "Show menu bar".

172

Windows Live Mail is a very basic email program, and users looking for more features and options will be better suited by programs such as Thunderbird and Eudora.

Back up Your Emails

The provision of email facilities is a very important function of the modern day computer, and just as people often like to keep personal letters, they also like to keep their emails. It is also an important means of business communication and these messages usually need to be kept as records.

Windows Live Mail provides an easy way to back up your messages and contacts.

1 From Windows Live Mail's File menu, select Export, Messages

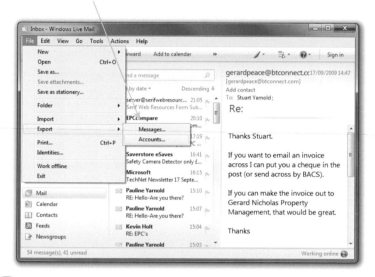

2 Select Microsoft Windows Live Mail

3 Browse to your backup folder and click Next

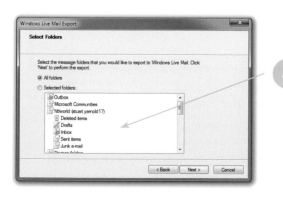

4 Select the email folders to back up, click Next and the backup will be created

173

Hot tip

If you just want to back up a particular message, double-click it and select Save As from the File menu. You can then save it where you like.

Hot tip

Should you ever lose your emails, you can restore them from the backup by selecting Import, Messages from the File menu.

Hot tip

Users of Microsoft Outlook can download an automatic backup utility at www.microsoft.com/downloads. Enter "personal folders backup" in the search box and click Go.

Back up Your Email Account

Backing up your email account is perhaps not as important as backing up your email messages because the account can be set up again if necessary. Nevertheless, it can be a nuisance, particularly if you have several accounts, as many people do.

Windows Live Mail makes it easy.

1 Click Tools on the menu bar and then Accounts

Hot tip

It's always a good idea to store backups on a separate medium. In the case of email account settings, which are very small files, a USB flash drive is ideal.

2 Select the account to be backed up and click Export

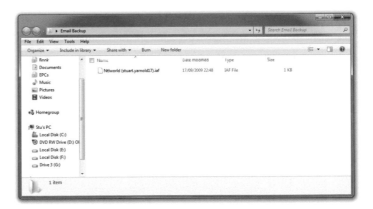

3 Browse to the backup folder and click Save

Should you ever need to reinstall the account, or accounts, simply reverse the above procedure, only this time click Import in Step 2.

Open Blocked Attachments

Viruses transmitted by email are almost always contained in an attachment to the email. However, the attachment must be opened by the user before the virus can be released.

To prevent this, Windows Live Mail has a virus protection feature that prevents any attachment that it considers unsafe from being opened. When this happens, you will see a red bar at the top of the email saying the file has been deactivated. An example of this is shown below:

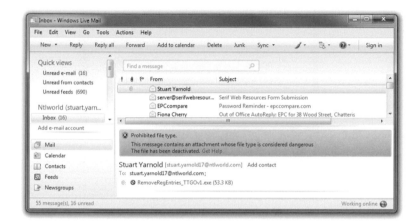

Don't forget

Be careful when opening attachments. This is the most common way for viruses to be transmitted. Before you open any attachment, take a look at its file extension and if it is of a dangerous type (see page 177), just delete it.

If you really want to read the message though, open it in plain text format – see the margin tip on page 176.

175

This is all very well and the feature will prevent people opening dangerous attachments, either through ignorance or carelessness. However, if you think an attachment is safe – you recognize the sender, for example – you need to know how to open it.

Also, if you share your email address only with people you trust, as many people do, you may want to disable the virus protection feature completely.

Do it as described below:

1   From Windows Live Mail's menu bar, click Tools, Safety Options

2   Click the Security tab

...cont'd

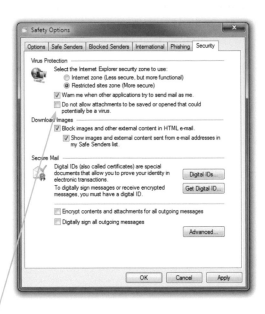

Hot tip

Windows Live Mail can be configured to read email in plain text format. When you enable this setting, no dangerous content in the email is run. Do it as follows:

• From the Tools menu, click Options

• Click the Read tab and then check the "Read all messages in plain text" check box

3 Uncheck the "Do not allow attachments to be saved or opened that could potentially be a virus" check box under Virus Protection and then click OK. Now you will be able to open the attachment

Of course, if you do decide to disable this protection feature, you run the risk of inadvertently opening a dangerous attachment. Therefore, you need to be able to recognize when one has arrived in your Inbox because Windows Live Mail is not going to warn you. To do this, look at the extension of the file in the attachment. This will be below the red warning bar, as shown below:

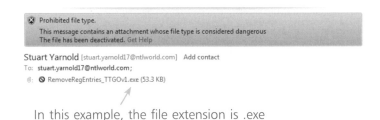

In this example, the file extension is .exe

Now refer to the tables on pages 177-178. These will show you which file extensions are safe to open and which are not. Once you are confident the file is OK, you can open the attachment.

High-Risk File Attachments

An email attachment ending in any of the file extensions in the table below can, potentially, be carrying a virus:

File Extension	Description
.ADE	Microsoft Access Project extension
.ADP	Microsoft Access Project
.BAS	Visual Basic Class module
.BAT	Batch file
.CHM	Compiled HTML help file
.CMD	Windows NT Command Script
.COM	MS-DOS application
.CPL	Control Panel extension
.CRT	Security certificate
.EXE	Application
.HLP	Windows help file
.HTA	HTML application
.INF	Setup information file
.INS	Internet communication settings
.ISP	Internet communication settings
.JS	JScript file
.JSE	JScript Encoded Script file
.LNK	Shortcut
.MDB	Microsoft Access application
.MDE	Microsoft Access MDE database
.MSC	Microsoft Common Console document
.MSI	Windows installer package
.MSP	Windows installer patch
.MST	Visual Test Source file
.PCD	Photo CD image
.PIF	Shortcut to MS-DOS program
.REG	Registry file
.SCR	Screensaver
SCT	Windows Script Component
.URL	Internet shortcut
.VB	VBScript file
.VBE	VBScript Encoded Script file
.VBS	VBScript Script file
.ZIP	Zipped folder

Beware

In an effort to disguise the extension of the file in which the virus is hidden, some virus writers give the file two extensions. The dangerous one is always the last. If you ever get such an attachment, delete it immediately.

177

Beware

An attachment extension to be particularly wary of is .zip. This catches many people out as most PC users are familiar with the Zip compression format and see no threat in it.

Low-Risk File Attachments

The file types in this table are extremely unlikely to be carrying a virus and can be considered to be safe:

File Extension	Description
.GIF	Picture - Graphics Interchange Format
.TIF or TIFF	Picture - Tagged Image File Format
.MPEG	Movie - Motion Picture Expert Group
.AVI	Movie - Audio Video Interleaved
.MP3	Sound - MPEG compressed audio
.WAV	Sound - Audio
.TXT or TEXT	Notepad document
.BMP	Picture - Windows Bitmap
.ICO	Picture - Icon
.PNG	Picture - Portable Network Graphic
.WMF	Picture - Windows Meta File
.LOG	Log file

Beware

Note that in general, image formats are considered to be safe. The exception to this is the JPEG format, which can carry a virus.

Open Blocked Images

Another security feature in Windows Live Mail prevents images included in web pages from being opened automatically. When this happens, the areas in the email message that contain images display a red X placeholder rather than the image itself.

There are two reasons for this:

1) It protects the user from potentially offensive material

2) It helps prevent spam. Many spammers include an image URL in their emails. This notifies the spammer when the message is opened, thus confirming that the address is real

Should the user wish to see the image, he or she just has to right-click and click Download Images. It is also possible to disable the feature so that all images are shown automatically when the message is opened.

Do this by clicking Tools on the menu bar and clicking Security Options. Then click the Security tab and uncheck "Block images and other external content in HTML email".

Global Email Access

Email has become a very important facet of our lives and, for many, it is well nigh essential – to the point of having to be able to access it wherever they may be.

The simplest way to have global access to your email is to use a web mail service, such as those provided by Google (Gmail) and Microsoft (Windows Live Hotmail). With these services, both sending and receiving email is done online rather than from a program on the PC. Furthermore, all messages are stored on the provider's server, which means they can be accessed from any PC, anywhere in the world.

The problem with web mail comes when an Internet connection is not available at the same time you need to access your saved messages. Because they are all online, you won't be able to.

The solution to this comes in the form of a little known option found in nearly all email programs that enables the user to save copies of their emails on their ISP's server. By doing so, email messages will be accessible both offline and online (globally). Furthermore, should you lose, or accidently delete, a message, you'll have a backup from which to restore it.

As Windows Live Mail is going be used by many people, we'll show you how to do it with this program:

1 On Windows Live Mail's menu bar, click Tools, Accounts

Don't forget

Another issue with web mail is the fact that many of the providers subject users to a bombardment of advertisments in return for a free account.

Indeed, many of them are known to trawl through users' messages so as to better target these ads.

179

...cont'd

2 Select your email account and click Properties

3 Click the Advanced tab and then check "Leave a copy of messages on server". Click Apply and you're done

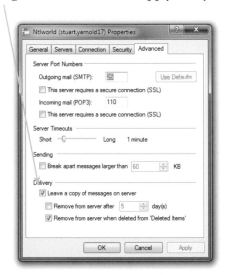

You'll now be able to manage your email from your PC, and also have access to it on your ISP's server from any computer. Very handy for checking your emails while on holiday.

A Spam-Free Inbox

Spam accounts for approximately three-quarters of email traffic worldwide. That adds up to several billion messages every day.

If you find yourself the recipient of an endless stream of advertisements, too good to be true offers, etc., what can you do about it?

The first step is to close your account and then set up a new one – this will stop it immediately. You then need to make sure the new account is kept out of the spammers' reach. Observing the following rules will help:

1) Make your address as long as possible. Among other things, spammers use automated generators that churn out millions of combinations (aaa@aol.com, aab@aol.com, and so on). It won't take them long to catch up with bob@aol.com

2) Never post your address on a website. Spammers use spiders that trawl the Web looking for the @ symbol, which is in all email addresses

3) If you need to give an address to access a web page, give a false one. Alternatively, set up a specific account with filters that direct all received emails to the deleted items folder. Use this account when an address is asked for

4) Never click the "Unsubscribe from this mailing list" link in a received email. This tells the spammer that your address is real and could open the floodgates

5) Make use of your email program's filters (Message Rules in Windows Live Mail). Properly configured, these can cut out a lot of spam

6) Use a Bayesian filter. This is available as a third-party product and integrates with your email program. Its effectiveness is due to the fact that it is "intelligent" and thus, can be trained in much in the same way as Voice Recognition software. The Bayesian filter examines all aspects of a message, as opposed to simple keyword checking that classifies a message as spam on the basis of a single word or phrase. Once set up and trained, a Bayesian filter will eliminate 99 per cent of spam

Hot tip

Once you are on the spammers' lists, the only way of stopping them is to close the account.

Beware

Chatrooms, Newsgroups and Message Boards are favorite places for spammers. Never post your email address on these websites.

Beware

Never reply to a spammer. If you do, you will confirm that your address is a real one.

Organize Your Emails

If you're like most people, your Inbox will be literally bulging at the seams with messages from weeks, months and even years ago. This tip shows how to tidy it up and then keep it tidy.

1 Create a new message folder for each of your contacts

2 Go through the Inbox and move your messages to the new categorized folders. Delete any you don't want

Having created order out of chaos, you need to make sure it stays that way, and without having to do it manually. To this end, you now need to set up your email program's message filters to do the job automatically.

3 From Windows Live Mail's Tools menu, select Message Rules, Mail

Hot tip

A big advantage of organizing your emails in this way is when you need to locate an old message for rereading. Instead of having to search through an over-flowing Inbox, you will know exactly where it is.

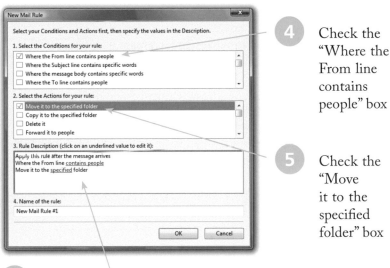

4 Check the "Where the From line contains people" box

5 Check the "Move it to the specified folder" box

6 Click "contains people" and in the dialog box that opens, enter a contact's email address. Then click "specified" and click the folder you created for the contact. Repeat the above procedure for all of your contacts

From this point on, all messages from the contacts you have specified will be moved automatically to the designated folders.

Automatic Picture Resizing

As anybody who regularly uses email will know, email programs allow users to either insert images directly into the email or attach them as a file.

The problem with this is that unless the image has been reduced in size in an imaging program (a process of which many people are unsure), it is possible to end up sending a huge picture file that will take the recipient ages to download. Most people find this extremely irritating, as it can occupy their connection for a considerable length of time. This is particularly so if they use a dial-up modem.

Windows saves the day with its Email Picture Resizing utility.

Hot tip

You can resize any number of pictures at the same time – you are not restricted to just one.

1 Right-click the image you want to send with your email, select Send To and then Mail Recipient

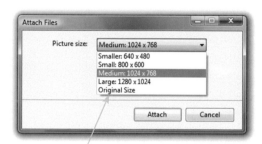

2 Select the required option, e.g. Small, Medium, Original Size, etc., and then click Attach

3 Click OK and an email message window will open with the resized image attached. All you have to do is type in the address and the text before sending the message

Beware

Be wary of using the Small, and Smaller, resize options. While these reduce the size of files enormously, they also reduce the quality of the images considerably.

A couple of things to be aware of are:

1) Pictures resized in this way are converted to the JPEG format, which you may or may not want

2) Some image formats (Photoshop's PSD, for example), cannot be converted by the utility, and thus cannot be resized. They will be attached to the email but at the original size

Email Receipt Confirmation

Email is a wonderful form of communication. Perhaps its only failing is that senders have no way of knowing if and when their messages have been read. Try the following:

1 On Windows Live Mail's toolbar, click Tools, Options. Then click the Receipts tab

Don't forget

Knowing if someone has read your email or not is extremely useful in many different situations. A typical example is when arranging meetings.

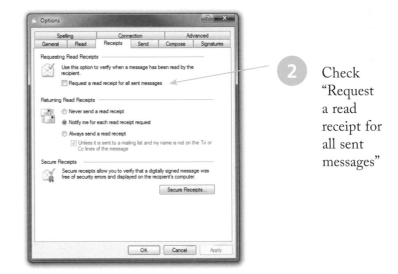

2 Check "Request a read receipt for all sent messages"

When the recipient receives the message, he/she is advised that a read receipt has been requested. However, there is no obligation to send one. If they do, fine; the sender knows it's been received. If they choose not to though (and most people don't) the sender is none the wiser. Thus, this method does have its limitations.

A better way is to take the decision out of the recipient's hands, i.e. confirmation is sent automatically. To set this up you will need a third-party utility. These are available on the Internet.

One that the author uses is MSGTAG. This is a free application available at www.msgtag.com. Once set up, the sender receives an email confirmation shortly after a message is opened at the other end. The recipient sees just a small MSGTAG footer stating that you've been notified of them having received the message.

Programs of this type work by adding a tag to sent emails. When the recipient opens it, the tag is activated and the program's server detects the unique code it contains and is thus able to identify the email. A confirmation (receipt) email is then sent to the sender.

Hot tip

The next time you get the old "I never received it" excuse, you'll be able to say "Well, actually, you did."

13 Multimedia

Multimedia has always been one of the most popular uses of PCs. Here, we look at various ways of enhancing your multimedia experience, and show you some recommended software.

Play Any Media File

Video and audio files in their raw state are huge in size. To make it easier to manage these files, e.g. downloading, copying, etc., compression techniques are used to reduce their size.

Hot tip

Most of the codec packs are designed for specific versions of Windows. If you do decide to install one, be sure it is compatible with the Windows version you are using.

The type of program that does the compressing is known as a codec and there are literally hundreds of them. Two well-known examples are DIVX for video and MP3 for audio.

However, once a file has been compressed, it must then be decompressed before it can be played. The decompression is done by the same codec that compressed the file originally.

This gives rise to a problem that has long plagued computer users; they have a media file but are unable to play it because the required codec is not installed on the PC.

There are a couple of ways to resolve this issue. One is to check the media file with a program that will analyze it and tell you which codec is required to play it. One such program is Gspot and we explain how to use it on page 137.

The second way is to download and install a codec pack, which contains codecs for virtually all the many types of media file. Note that while Windows 7 provides the most commonly used codecs, there are still many that it does not.

There are quite a few of these codec packs available on the Internet and if you decide to go down this route, we suggest you do a bit of reseach before actually installing one. Some of them can cause more problems than they solve.

One codec pack that the author has evaluated and found to be good is the Win7codecs pack. You can download it from http://shark007.net/win7codecs.html.

This application does just what it says on the can; it installs all the codecs you are ever likely to need, without also installing any superfluous features, such as bundled media players, etc.

Build a Home Entertainment Center

One of the reasons that Home Entertainment Centers (HECs) are becoming so popular is that they combine all the devices necessary to keep the average family entertained into a single unit. Not only does this save space, they only need one power point and there are no complex connection issues. Another is that all the various functions can be operated with a single remote control.

Unfortunately, these systems are not cheap. So rather than shell out megabucks to replace a perfectly good collection of stand-alone devices, consider building one around the PC instead.

Requirements

The modern computer provides most of the hardware needed to build a basic HEC. You've got a monitor to watch TV and video, a DVD player to play CDs and DVDs, and speakers to listen to music. The only other things you'll need are a TV/radio tuner, and suitable software to integrate and control the devices.

Owners of high-end versions of Windows 7 PCs already have the software in the form of Windows Media Center (WMC) and so, for an outlay of about $100 for a decent TV/radio tuner with a remote control, will be ready to go. All they have to do is install the TV tuner and then run WMC's setup wizard.

Considerations

The problem with the basic setup described above is that PCs are inherently unsuitable for use in a living room, which is where the HEC will be used. They are noisy and usually nothing much to look at. If you can live with these limitations though, there's nothing holding you back. Move the PC into the living room and, with the aid of the remote control, you'll be able to watch/record TV, play your music and videos, look at your photos, and even browse the Internet (if your monitor or TV is large enough) without ever leaving your armchair.

However, for the reasons mentioned above, you may not wish to have the PC in the living room. Alternatively, you may want to build a more sophisticated system that can be used in more than one room. In either case, you will have to incorporate your HEC devices into a network.

Hot tip

The beauty of an HEC is that everything can be operated with a single remote control.

Hot tip

If you have a large-screen LCD TV, it should have a DVI or VGA connection that enables you to hook it up to the PC in place of the monitor. Note that this will require a video card capable of supplying the high resolutions needed by large-screen displays.

...cont'd

Hot tip

An extender connects a device to a network, enables it to access the media content of the PC, and allows it to be remotely controlled.

Beware

A connection found on most PC video cards and consumer TVs is S-Video. While this provides a high quality signal, it cannot support HDTV.

Hot tip

A simple way of creating a wired network is to use HomePlug. This system uses the telephone wiring in the house to form the network.

Networked HECs

In a networked HEC, each device (TV, Hi-Fi system, etc.) is connected to the PC via a Media Extender (see margin note). The connections are made in one of two ways:

1) Network cable – this is known as a wired network and uses network cable (available from any good PC store) with Ethernet plugs at each end. These plug into Ethernet sockets on both the PC and the extenders

2) Radio link – this is known as a wireless network as the devices are connected by a radio frequency. In this setup, the PC has a wireless network adapter, and the extenders are wireless versions to which the devices are connected by an Ethernet cable. The network is set up using the Windows Network wizard (available from the Network and Sharing Center in the Control Panel)

Of the two types, a wired network is the best option in terms of performance and reliability. It does, however, require cables to be run to wherever a networked device is to be located. Wireless networks are much easier to set up as there is no cabling involved, and are also much more versatile as the devices can be moved to wherever they are required on an as-and-when basis.

Connections

Whichever option you go for, it will be necessary to make some physical connections, e.g. TV to PC, TV to extender, etc. For a high quality picture, a DVI connection is recommended. This will be found on any modern video card, extender, and most LCD TVs. A VGA connection will also be acceptable. HD Component Video works well but is not commonly found on PCs. All of these connections can support high-definition TV (HDTV).

Applications

By connecting your HEC devices to a network via an extender, you can use them in any location. The extender's remote control will enable you to access any type of media on the PC, wherever it is situated.

You can also incorporate other types of device in the network to extend its range of uses. For example, it is quite simple to set up a home surveillance system by adding cameras to the network.

Keep the Discs in the Drawer

One of the most irritating things about playing games on a computer is the constant need to insert and change discs. This can also be the eventual cause of physical damage to the discs.

While most game manufacturers allow their games to be run directly from the hard drive, thus eliminating the need to use the discs, there are still some that don't. Some people try to get round this by copying the disc to the hard drive and then installing the game from there. Unfortunately, this rarely works – when you try to run the game you usually get a "No disk in CD drive" error message. This is manufacturers' copy protection at work.

The solution to the problem is a virtual drive. This is an emulated drive created and controlled by a program. The user creates an image of the game's disc on the hard drive, which can be played in the virtual drive; the real disc is not required at all.

There are many of these applications available on the Internet. A good one is CD Space, available at http://en.cdspace.com You can either buy the full version or try out a time-limited version.

Hot tip

Virtual drives can be used with any type of program; they are not restricted to games. Although most applications now offer an "install to disk" option, there are still many that do not. A virtual drive is the answer.

189

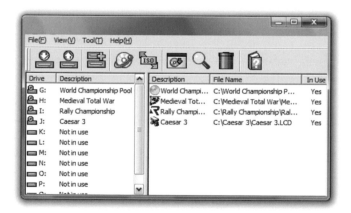

Virtual drives   Installed games

Hot tip

Most CD/DVD authoring programs also provide a virtual CD drive. With these though, you will only have one drive.

Virtual drive programs can create up to 23 virtual drives, which means you can have up to 23 different games pre-loaded and ready to go. You can put the discs in a drawer and forget about them. Also, as the games are being played from the hard drive, they will perform better.

Another advantage of these programs is that they can override most manufacturers' copy protection methods.

Graphic Formats Unravelled

When using graphics files in documents, presentations, web pages, or for printing, it is important that you choose a format that is suitable for the task in hand. Using the wrong one can result in poor quality images, images that take an eternity to open, or images with unnecessarily high file sizes.

The first thing to realize is that image formats are split into two main groups: Vector and Raster.

Vector

Vector images are composed of mathematically-defined geometric shapes, e.g. lines, squares, circles, etc., and are typically generated by drawing applications such as Adobe Illustrator and Microsoft Visio. Two notable advantages of this format are:

1) Image size can be increased to an almost unlimited degree without noticeable loss of image quality

2) Individual parts of an image can be edited. For example, if a particular image contains both text and objects, it is possible to change the text's formatting (font, color, size, etc.)

Vector formats tend to be proprietary, i.e. specific to a particular program. However, many drawing applications allow you to save an image in formats used by other popular vector programs.

Commonly used vector formats include:

- WMF – this is the standard vector file used in Microsoft products, such as Microsoft Office

- PCT – this is the standard vector format used by Macintosh operating systems

- EPS – this format can be used on a variety of platforms, including Macintosh and Windows

Raster

In raster files, the image is comprised of a grid, or matrix, of tiny squares called pixels. This allows extremely complex pictures to be recorded, typically photographs, and it's this characteristic that makes them the most widely used format.

Hot tip

Windows 7 includes support for a recent Microsoft image format known as Windows Media Photo (WMP). This is an advance on the JPEG format that will, it is claimed, offer the same quality at half the file size.

Hot tip

Many of the vector formats (including the three mentioned on the right), can also handle raster data. These are often called Metafiles.

The main drawback is that in their raw state, they can be very large files. However, this is compensated for by the fact that this format can be heavily compressed to reduce file size.

With regard to compression, there are two types, lossy and lossless:

1) Lossy – with this method, unnecessary data is permanently stripped out of the file, thus reducing its size. Although it may be imperceptible, the quality of the image is reduced

2) Lossless – here, data is temporarily removed from the file. When the file is opened, the data is replaced. Thus, there is no loss of image quality

Commonly used raster formats are:

- JPEG – a lossy format, JPEG's main advantage is the fact that it can be highly compressed. This makes it ideal for use in web pages, and where a low file size is required. It can also handle 24-bit color, and so can be used for professional printing (although there are better formats for this)

- GIF – this is a low-size lossless image format, which is mostly found on websites where it is used for small low-quality images, such as advertising banners, clip art, etc. Use this format if you want the lowest possible file size and the quality of the image is not important

- PNG – this is an advanced version of the GIF format and it offers several advantages, such as better color support and compression. PNGs are lossless

- TIFF – this is a lossless format offering features that make it the ideal format for professional printing. File sizes are high but image quality is excellent

Summary

For web pages where quality is not important, or low file size is, use GIF or PNG. Otherwise, use JPEG.

For general computer use, e.g. storing and viewing your holiday snaps, JPEG is the recommended format.

For professional printing of photographs, use the TIFF format.

Hot tip

There are several variants of the JPEG format. These include: JP2000, JPM, and JP3D. These are designed for more specific uses, such as volumetric imaging (JP3D), and usually require a plug-in.

Hot tip

If an image contains both drawing objects (vector) and photographs (raster), use a metafile format such as EPS.

Editing Your Photos

Hot tip

If you have an image that cannot be replaced, make a copy and use that for editing. If you mess it up, you've still got the original.

Hot tip

Before you edit a photo, convert it to a TIFF file first. This can be done with the editing program. Then reopen it to start editing.

Hot tip

The imaging program provided by Windows is Windows Photo Viewer. Unfortunately, it doesn't provide any editing features. If you're serious about your photos, we suggest you acquire Corel Paintshop Pro, or a program with similar capabilities.

Calibrate the Monitor

The first thing you must do is calibrate the monitor. If it is incorrectly set up, no matter how carefully you edit your images, when you print them, or view them on a different monitor, they will look different. You may even make them worse.

Calibration software should be bundled with your monitor. If not, use the calibration utility provided by Windows 7 – see page 122.

Covert the Image to a Lossless Format

As we saw on page 191, image formats are either lossy or lossless. Every time a lossy image is edited, some loss of image data occurs. Thus, the more times it is edited, the worse the end result. Lossless images, on the other hand, can be edited any number of times with no loss of quality.

So before you edit any image of the lossy type, convert it to a TIFF, which is lossless. Having edited the image, convert it back to the original file type. This ensures that the original image quality is retained.

Brightness and Contrast Adjustments

All image editors provide brightness and contrast controls. Many also have an auto one-click setting that does the job automatically. While both can work well, often the result is less than optimal.

A better, and more reliable, way is to use the image editor's Histogram control. This presents a graphical representation of the image showing its color distribution in terms of brightness and darkness. The left of the graph represents black and the right represents white.

Consider the following example of a badly under-exposed picture:

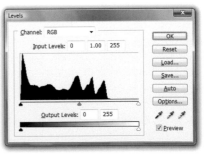

The image's Histogram shows that its data is over to the left of the graph, i.e. its dark tones are overemphasized (if an image's exposure is correct, the data will be centered in the graph).

Don't forget

The pointer on the right controls light tones (highlights), the one on the left controls dark tones (shadows), and the middle one controls midtones (contrast).

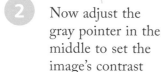

1 Drag the white pointer to where the data begins. This sets the image's exposure to the correct level

2 Now adjust the gray pointer in the middle to set the image's contrast

Hot tip

If an image is over-exposed, its data will be to the right of the graph. In this case, you would drag the black slider to where the data begins.

Color Correction

The next adjustment to make is to the image's colors. This is done with the Hue/Saturation control (shown below). A common mistake is to adjust all the colors simultaneously until the picture "looks about right". However, this often results in one color being correct and the others being incorrect.

The right way to do it is to edit each color individually by selecting it from the Edit menu. Adjustments will thus affect that color only.

An example is shown on the next page.

Hot tip

Another, more advanced, tool that can be used for color correction is the Curves tool.

...cont'd

Hot tip

Another way to adjust the color of a specific area of an image is to select the area with a selection tool such as the Marquee or Lasso tool. Any changes you make will affect the selected area only.

In this image, the grass and trees have a yellowish tint that gives a slightly washed-out or faded look

Adjusting green only gives the grass and trees a more natural color, while the other colors remain unchanged

Color Cast Correction

A common problem with digital photos is the image having a tinted cast. This can also be corrected with the Hue/Saturation control. Select the color of the cast in the Edit menu and then drag the slider back to eliminate it.

Sharpening

The first rule of image sharpening is that this process is the last edit to be made. The second rule is to ignore the Sharpen and Sharpen More tools, as they provide little user control and usually result in the image being sharpened incorrectly.

Hot tip

Sharpening tools should be used with restraint. Over-using them will ruin your images.

The tool you should use is the Unsharp Mask. When using this, you need to zoom in closely so that you can work with precision.

Many imaging programs provide a zoom-in preview window for this purpose. If yours doesn't, use the program's zoom control to get in close.

The rule of thumb is to look for halos along sharp edges. When you see these, reduce the Threshold setting until the halos disappear. Then you should be about right.

Game Play Optimization

The average computer system is not specified highly enough to play many of today's 3D games at their optimum level. By this we mean all sound/graphic enhancements and features turned on and set at maximum. With "all guns blazing" many of the games will struggle, with gameplay being slow and jerky.

The following tips will help to prevent this:

1) Reinstall the game and choose the option that installs the majority (or all) of the game's data on the hard drive. The less the game has to access the disc, the more smoothly it will run

2) Before you start the game, switch the PC off for a few seconds. Doing this will clear the memory and ensure the PC is in an optimal condition

3) When playing the game make sure no other applications are running on the PC

4) Try reducing the amount of action, e.g. reduce the number of opponents, cars in a racing game, etc. The less that is going on, the better the PC will be able to cope with the game

5) Go into the game's graphics setup options and reduce the screen resolution. Then reduce settings such as Anti-Aliasing, Shadows, and Textures. These features improve graphic quality considerably but do place a heavy load on the PC

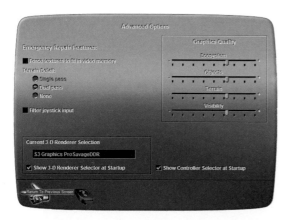

Graphics options for MotoCross Madness 2. Dragging the sliders back will speed up the game

6) The final, and most drastic, option is to upgrade your system's hardware, i.e. the memory, and possibly the CPU and video system as well

195

Hot tip

Before buying any 3D game, make sure your CPU and memory match its recommended system requirements. These will be somewhere on the box. You must also have the version of DirectX required by the game; otherwise it won't run properly, if at all.

Don't forget

Achieving a smooth level of gameplay is usually a compromise between graphics quality and performance, and will require a certain amount of trial and error.

Hot tip

If the game's installation options allow you to install the entire game to the hard drive, do so. Having to constantly retrieve data from the CD/DVD drive can cause the game to stutter.

Turn Your PC Into a TV/Video Recorder

TV tuner hardware has advanced a long way since its early days, and it's now possible to buy these devices in the form of tiny flash drives that plug into a USB port. These often incorporate two tuners that allow you to watch one program while recording another.

What hasn't advanced is the software usually supplied with these devices, much of which is truly awful. The author recently bought a TV tuner from one of the leading manufacturers in this field and found that while the device itself was superb, the software was virtually unusable. For example, recorded programs when played back were jerky and dropped frames, while the electronic program guide (EPG) simply didn't work at all. So all it was good for was watching TV and nothing else.

The solution was to delete the bundled software from the PC and switch to Windows Media Center. This is a superb program that fully utilizes the capabilities of modern TV tuner hardware.

WMC instantly recognizes the TV hardware the first time you run it after installing the device, and then opens a setup wizard that automatically scans for available channels and configures the device. This is all done so effortlessly that it is difficult to understand why the bundled software is so slow and problematic.

Once set up, watching and recording TV with WMC is a breeze.

Hot tip

TV tuners come in two types: analog and digital. Of the two, digital is the recommended option as it does not suffer from interference, e.g. ghosting.

TV options in Windows Media Center

Click Live TV and you can watch any channel either full-screen or in a resizable window. A range of options and features, including a record button, are available at the bottom-right.

The recorded TV window shows a list of all the programs you have recorded together with useful information, such as the date of recording, channel it was recorded on, plus a brief or full outline of the plot, depending on which view you select. The latter is extremely useful when browsing programs recorded some time ago, the details of which you may have forgotten.

The electronic program guide (EPG) is probably the most useful feature of all. This updates automatically and allows you to look days ahead to see what programs are coming.

If you find one you wish to record, even if it's not due for several days, simply right-click and select Record. WMC will do the rest. Playback quality is smooth with none of the jerkiness found with other software. Image quality is excellent as well.

Multimedia Viewers

For viewing your pictures, Windows 7 provides Windows Photo Viewer. While this program is adequate, it does have a very limited set of features. A much better application is IrfanView.

Hot tip

Irfanview's already wide range of functions can be further extended by downloading free plug-ins from the manufacturer's website.

This is a powerful imaging program that has a wide range of features; far too many to list here. Quite simply, no computer user should be without it. IrfanView is available as a free download at www.irfanview.com.

With regard to video, Windows 7's offering is Windows Media Player. This is an excellent program that, unlike Photo Viewer, has a good range of features and capabilities. So much so, in fact, that it can be a difficult application to get to grips with.

For users who just want a simple, no-frills utility to watch their videos, we recommend the Zoom Player (standard version), available as a free download from www.inmatrix.com.

Don't forget

Irfanview and Zoom Player are both completely free of spyware and adware.

This video player has a clean, uncluttered interface, is very quick to load, yet has a powerful set of features.

For a free application, it's unbeatable.

14 Miscellaneous

This chapter contains a number of tips that relate to both the PC and the Internet. For example, a particularly useful tip demonstrates how to get free online storage space. We also look at some handy applications that may not be apparent at first glance.

Keyboard Calculator

The calculator provided by Windows is a very handy and much-used application. However, operating it with a mouse is less than ideal as it is very easy to press the wrong button. You could never add up a column of figures at anything like the speed it could be done with a real calculator.

The tip described below allows you to do just that.

1 Press the Num Lock key on the keyboard

2 Open the calculator by going to Start, All Programs, Accessories, Calculator (you can also type calc in the Start Menu search box)

3 Instead of fiddling about with the mouse to enter numbers, simply use the numeric keypad on the keyboard

Key	Action
/	The equivalent of divide
*	The equivalent of multiply
+	The equivalent of plus
-	The equivalent of minus
Enter	The equivalent of equals

Don't forget

Windows calculator can be expanded to a scientific mode. Select this option from the View menu.

Hot tip

While the calculator supplied by Windows is perfectly adequate for most needs, there are many more specialized calculators available for download from the Internet.

200

Restart Windows Explorer

From time to time Windows Explorer, which is the application responsible for the Taskbar, Desktop and Start Menu, will crash. The result is that the Taskbar and all the Desktop icons will disappear leaving a blank screen. With nothing to click, the user seemingly has no options with which to recover.

The solution is as follows:

Hot tip

To open the Task Manager when you have no access to the Taskbar, press Ctrl+Shift+Esc.

1   Press Ctrl+Shift+Esc. This opens the Task Manager

2   From the File menu, click New Task (Run...)

3   In the Open box, type explorer and then click OK

Windows will now restart Windows Explorer, which will in turn, reinstate the Taskbar, Start Menu and the Desktop icons.

Turbo-Charge the Mouse

Many users are not aware that there are several aspects of the mouse that can be enhanced, both visually and operationally.

Pointer Speed

The first is the speed at which the pointer moves across the screen. The default setting is fine for most users but some, gamers for example, will benefit from a faster speed.

Hot tip

Clicking the Pointers tab will give you access to a range of mouse pointers. Have a look here because you may find pointers that are more suitable for your use of the PC than the default pointer.

 Go to Start, Control Panel and click Mouse. Then click the Pointer Options tab

Drag the slider forward to increase the pointer's speed

Mouse Snap To

While you have the Pointer Options dialog box open, you can alter another setting that will change the mouse's behavior.

Enabling Snap To will eliminate the need to move your mouse to a certain extent, by making the pointer jump automatically to the default button whenever a new dialog box is opened.

Some people love this; others hate it. Give it a try.

Hot tip

Have you ever been in a situation where you have simply lost the pointer? Checking "Show location of pointer when I press the CTRL key" will enable you to find it instantly the next time.

Easy Reading

ClearType is a feature that was introduced in Windows XP, and is an anti-aliasing technique that smooths the edges of fonts, thus making them easier to read.

With XP, the feature was disabled by default; with Windows 7 the default setting is on. However, not many users are aware that they can tweak the level of ClearType. This can be done as described below:

1 Go to Start, Control Panel and click Display. On the left, click "Adjust ClearType text"

2 At the first screen, click Next. At the second, select the monitor to apply the settings to (assuming you have more than one)

3 The next four screens will present you with different ClearType options

Hot tip

Not everybody likes ClearType. If you want to disable it, go to Start, Control Panel and click Display. On the left, click "Adjust ClearType text". Then uncheck "Turn on ClearType".

Hot tip

If you have more than one monitor, you can apply different ClearType settings to each one.

4 Choose the setting that's best for you, click Next and then Finish

Get an Online Hard Drive

An online hard drive is basically a chunk of cyberspace allocated to a user, which he or she can use to store data. There are many websites that provide this service and most of them offer a small amount of storage space for a nominal fee, or even for free. Larger amounts cost more.

For example, the author has an account with IDrive (www.idrive. com), which provides him with 2 GB of storage space absolutely free. He has used this to store copies of all his books, emails, documents, photos and Internet Favorites, as shown below:

Hot tip

By using several of these websites, you can build up a large amount of online space without parting with a cent.

Hot tip

Other online storage websites that you can try, include:

• www.box.net
  (1 GB free)
• www.freedrive.com
  (5 GB free)
• www.esnips.com
  (1 GB free)

The most obvious advantage of storing data online is security. If your hard drive fails, you can download the data to the new drive; thus, it can never be lost.

Another advantage is that the data can be accessed from any PC. If you're on holiday, for example, you can access your online data from an Internet Cafe. If you're on a business trip, it can be accessed from a laptop.

Yet another use is file sharing. If you want to send a friend a file, or even a program, simply upload it to your online storage space and then they can download it from their end.

Hot tip

Once you've got your data online, you can arrange and organize it just as you would with a real hard drive. Most online storage websites provide a File Manager for this purpose.

Give Your PC a Free Tune-Up

Many users like to keep tabs on their PC's performance. While Windows provides several tools for this purpose, they are far from straightforward and thus only suitable for more advanced users.

Those of you who like things simple have an easier way. There are quite a few websites that offer system performance evaluators and optimizers. One of the best is PCPitstop (www.pcpitstop.com). Visit this website and you will be able to give your system a complete health check.

Hot tip

Many of the tools at PCPitstop can be downloaded to the PC and run when required.

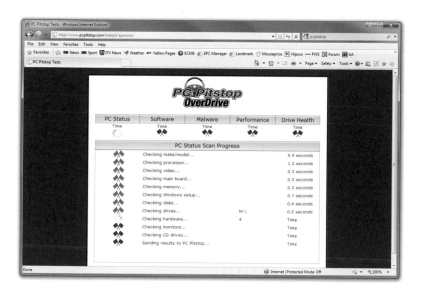

The screenshot above shows the author's PC being scanned with PCPitstops Tune-Up utility.

Other tools include system optimization, virus and malware checkers, Internet connection speed detection and optimization, and a privacy scanner that detects and deletes any information that can reveal what you've been doing on the PC and the Internet.

While we're not saying PCPitstop and similar websites are the answer to all your computer-related problems, they do provide a very simple and convenient way of checking out your system and repairing many common problems.

Hot tip

On a very similar note, Microsoft have the Windows Live OneCare utility, which can also be run from the Internet. This utility checks for viruses/malware, and also offers system cleanup and optimization tools.

Be on Time With Windows

Windows timekeeping utility has two cool features that many users will find useful:

Additional Clocks

The first one enables you to have up to three clocks all set to different time zones.

Don't forget

Users interested in timekeeping also have the Clock gadget to play with – see page 140.

1 Click the clock in the Notification Area and then click "Change date and time settings"

2 Click the Additional Clocks tab

3 Using the drop-down boxes, select the time zones you want for each clock. Then enter a display name

4 Hover the pointer over the system clock to see all the clocks

5 Click the system clock to see a larger view, plus the calendar

Reset the Clock Accurately

The usual method of resetting the PC's clock involves clicking little arrows, which is fiddly. There's also no guarantee that your reference clock is accurate. Windows provides an easier way that is also extremely accurate.

Hot tip

The Internet Time utility automatically synchronizes the time on your computer with Microsoft's time server; time.windows. com. This server is in turn synchronized with National Institute of Standards and Technology (NIST) computers, which are synchronized with an atomic clock.

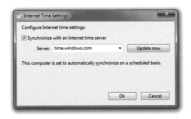

Repeat Step 1 above and then click the Internet Time tab. Click Change Settings and from the drop-down box, select a time server. Then click the Update Now button.

All the servers are synchronized with an atomic clock, and so are guaranteed to be accurate.

Single-Click Operation

A very simple tweak that many people are not aware of enables
an item to be opened with a single-click as opposed to the
default two.

1 Go to Start, Control Panel and open Folder Options

Hot tip

Single-click operation
also saves you having to
click an item in order to
select it. Simply position
the pointer over a file
and it will be selected
automatically.

3 Tick "Single-click to open an item" and then click OK.
Double-clicking will now be a thing of the past

Keep a Journal

Hot tip

Windows Journal is not available in all versions of Windows 7.

Windows Journal is a note-taking accessory that is intended primarily for use with Tablet PCs. It allows users of this type of PC to input data with an electronic pen, which can then be saved as files, converted to text, and edited in a word-processor, etc.

However, it is such a versatile application that it can be put to many other uses as well. To open a journal, right-click the Desktop and click New, Journal Document.

By default, it is set up for use with an electronic pen. However, by inserting resizable text boxes, you can input data with the keyboard. You can also insert pictures as shown below where the author has used the journal for researching holiday villas.

Hot tip

A useful application for Windows Journal is keeping a diary.

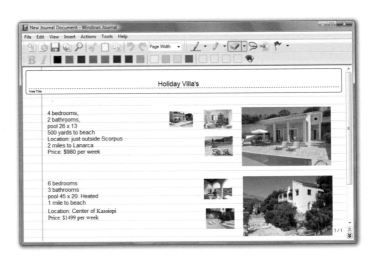

Windows Journal comes with a range of templates that enable the user to create and save customized journals for specific purposes. For example: taking notes, to-do lists, memos, etc.

Hot tip

Windows Journal can be also used as a substitute for Notepad, and provides more features and options when used for this purpose.

 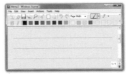 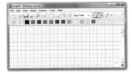

Journals can also be customized in terms of page layout, page background (colors, pictures), page views, text color, font and size. The pen tools enable the user to add annotation lines and text to graphics.

Windows Live Free Software

Online distribution of software is widely seen as the future of computing because the applications are available anywhere and at any time. All that's needed is an Internet connection. Furthermore, you don't even need to download them, they can be installed directly from the server.

"Windows Live" is Microsoft's attempt to take advantage of this developing trend, and the term is a collective name for a large number of mostly online applications and services that are now being provided by Microsoft.

The following applications are just some of the ones available online:

- Windows Live OneCare
- Windows Live OneCare Safety Scanner
- Windows Live Admin Center
- Windows Live ID
- Windows Live Local
- Windows Live Mail Mobile
- Windows Live Messenger
- Windows Live Spaces
- Windows Live Search (also known as Bing)
- Windows Live Toolbar
- Windows Live SkyDrive

Microsoft is also offering Office Live. This provides you with an online hard drive in which you can store up to 25 GB of data, plus online versions of Word, Excel, PowerPoint, and OneNote.

Also on offer is Office Live Small Business. This provides you with everything you need to build a website that is hosted by Microsoft for free.

Continuing the "Live" theme is Windows Live Essentials, which is a suite of applications that can be downloaded to the user's PC. These include Live Mail (an updated version of the Windows Mail email program provided with Windows Vista), Writer (a simple word processor), Messenger (a replacement for the old Windows Messenger), Photo Gallery and Movie Maker (for viewing and editing your photos and movies), Family Safety (shielding your kids from Internet dangers), and a browser toolbar that enables you to access all the Windows Live applications.

Hot tip

Others, notably Google and Yahoo, are getting in on the act. Many of the applications available from Windows Live are also available from these companies.

Hot tip

Get the Windows Live Essentials suite from http://download.live.com.

Useful Windows Utilities

Windows comes with many applications that may not be apparent initially. The following are two particularly useful tools:

Compressed Folders

Compression is a method of reducing the size of a file. Its main use is in the transportation of data via the Internet; the smaller the file, the quicker its upload/download time. Another use is to fit more data on removable media. This is extremely useful when making large-scale backups, or transferring data between PCs, for example.

Windows compression utility is very simple to use. Simply right-click the file or folder to be compressed and select Send To, Compressed (zipped folder). A special folder will be created in which the file is placed and automatically compressed.

Another way is to right-click the Desktop and select New, Compressed (zipped) Folder. An empty folder will be created; files can now be dragged to this folder where they will be compressed.

Snipping Tool

The Print Screen key is used to take a screenshot of whatever happens to be on the screen. Pressing it in conjunction with the Alt key takes one of the active window. To use the screenshot, it then has to be copied into an imaging program.

Windows Snipping tool (Start, All Programs, Accessories) not only simplifies the process but also provides many more options.

These include:

- Freeform snips
- Rectangular snips
- Window snips
- Full-screen snips

Having taken a snip, you can annotate it using a choice of colored pens, copy it to the clipboard, send it to your email program, or save it as a PNG, GIF, JPEG or HTML file.

Users who frequently use the Print Screen key will find Windows Snipping tool to be a vast improvement.

Don't forget

Compression is most effective when used with text files and can reduce the size of this type of file by some 50 per cent. Graphics files will typically be reduced by about 10 per cent.

Hot tip

A big advantage of the Snipping tool over the Print key option, is that screenshots can be saved in commonly used file types.

Don't forget

The Snipping tool is not available in all versions of Windows 7.

Index

N

O

P

R

S